UNDERSTANDING THE GOSPEL OF JOHN

Arthur H. Maynard

The Edwin Mellen Press
Lewiston/Queenston/Lampeter

Library of Congress Cataloging-in-Publication Data

Maynard, Arthur H.
  Understanding the Gospel of John / Arthur H. Maynard.
     p.   cm.
  Includes bibliographical references and indexes.
  ISBN 0-7734-9640-8
  1. Bible. N.T. John--Criticism, interpretation, etc. I. Title.
BS2615.2.M39 1991
226.5'06--dc20   91-37589
                                                                            CIP

A CIP catalog record for this book
is available from the British Library.

Scripture quotations, except where otherwise indicated, are from the Revised Standard Version Bible, copyright 1946, 1952, 1971 by the Division of Christian Education of the National Council of the Churches of Christ in the USA. Used by permission.

The Edwin Mellen Press   The Edwin Mellen Press
Box 450   Box 67
Lewiston, New York   Queenston, Ontario
USA 14092   CANADA L0S 1L0

              The Edwin Mellen Press, Ltd.
                   Lampeter, Dyfed, Wales
              UNITED KINGDOM SA48 7DY

          Printed in the United States of America

This book is dedicated to my wife,

Paula,

whose constant love, support and encouragement
made possible the writing and the
research reflected in it.

TABLE OF CONTENTS

Chapter I

The Gospel of the Johannine Church

The Gospel of John is one of the best loved parts of the New Testament. It is probably the favorite of more people than any other gospel. It is always the first to be translated into a foreign language whenever missionaries are working in the various parts of the world and they begin to get translations in the indigenous language. It is also the gospel about which there are radical differences of opinion among the scholars and on which a great deal of research has been done.

Traditionally this gospel is believed to have been written by John the Apostle, son of Zebedee, brother of-- the Apostle James, a Galilean fisherman before he became a disciple. But there are a number of problems with this view. It rests almost entirely on implications which are made in John 21, the last chapter of the book, which is almost universally regarded as an appendix written later than the gospel. If one looks at the end of chapter 20 there is a perfect ending: ". . .these are written that you may believe that Jesus is the Christ, the Son of God, and that believing you may have life in his name" (20:31). But this is followed by chapter 21 which seems to have been added for a couple of reasons, one of which was to make the gospel acceptable to the larger church and, in order to do that, to infer apostolic authorship, because one of the criteria by which the early church accepted and rejected books was apostolic authorship.

However, chapter 21 does not state apostolic authorship, it only infers it, and there are numerous problems with the idea that John, son of Zebedee, wrote this gospel. The author wrote in Greek and he not only wrote in Greek, he knew the Greek mind. The parables, those stories that Jesus told, which are recorded in Matthew, Mark and Luke, are absent in John. It would seem very, very probable that Jesus told parables--that it was his major method of teaching, the typical Jewish teaching method in that day--but in the Gospel of John the parables disappear and are replaced by dialogues. The dialogue was particularly a Greek method of writing. Most famous of the Greek writers of dialogue was Plato, but it was a form which was widely used, and with which any Greek reader would feel very much at home. The Johannine dialogues are based on ambiguous words. Jesus said something and his hearers always misunderstood. Now, people can be stupid, but they are not always stupid. But the people with whom Jesus has dialogue in this gospel are always stupid. Because they do always misunderstand him, I call these "conversations with the spiritually dull," and will look at some of them in detail later on. In these dialogues forty-six ambiguous words are used,[1] with the dialogue partner always misunderstanding Jesus' meaning. Now Jesus taught in Aramaic, in all probability. We do not know whether he knew Greek or not. Some scholars think he did. But the probability is that if he did know it, he did not use it in his teaching. Aramaic was the common language of Palestine in the time of Jesus, but there are not forty-six ambiguous words in Aramaic that can be translated to forty-six ambiguous words in Greek. There are about two that are ambiguous in the same way in Aramaic as they are in Greek. Furthermore, even if there were that many ambiguous words in Aramaic, it is almost inconceivable that any translator would be aware of them. So clearly the author knew Greek, he had a Greek style of writing, and this would hardly be true of a Galilean fisherman.

Further, the author of the Fourth Gospel reinterprets Jesus in a way in which an eyewitness would not be likely to do. One can compare the four gospels to a newspaper: Matthew, Mark and Luke are the reporters and John is the editorial writer. Now, if you think there is no editorial slanting going on in the news pages just compare the *Christian Science Monitor* with the *San Francisco Chronicle* or any other paper and see the difference in perspective. The first three gospel writers have a perspective that they want to get across, but they are primarily trying to report what happened, while

John is not really concerned with reporting what happened so much as he is with interpreting the events and trying to indicate their significance.

The first three gospels present Jesus as a messianic king, who was the descendent of the House of David. In John's gospel this is replaced with the pre-existent Logos. Logos translates as "word." "In the beginning was the word." By Logos the Greeks meant the reason that was behind the universe. The Logos was the order, the reason that was evident in the universe. But remember in the first chapter of Genesis God created by speaking: "God said, 'Let there be light'; and there was light" (Gen. 1:3). And so in Genesis there is also the idea of the Word. In John's Gospel, the Word is the creative force: "In the beginning was the Word, and the Word was with God, and the Word was God. He was in the beginning with God; all things were made through him, and without him was not anything made that was made" (John 1:1-3). So whether this idea of the Logos comes from Greek sources or whether it comes from Jewish sources is open to debate, but it is not the kind of reinterpretation that one would expect from a Galilean fisherman. A Galilean fisherman who walked with Jesus during his ministry would be much more inclined to report what he had seen and heard than to reinterpret Jesus in this kind of terminology.

The author also reinterprets the message of Jesus. In the first three, also called the Synoptic, gospels, the primary idea is the Kingdom of God, or as Matthew puts it, the Kingdom of Heaven, but this idea almost disappears in John. John has the term about three times.[2] The Kingdom of God had three major ideas connected with it in synoptic thought. One is the idea of the return of Christ. In John's Gospel Christ has already returned in the gift of the comforter. The second idea is the resurrection of the dead.[3] In John's Gospel this idea is replaced by the idea of eternal life, which is something that one enters into here and now, as one accepts Jesus. The story of Lazarus is the place where John's gospel makes the point most clearly. The idea associated with the Kingdom of God is the idea of the final judgment which in the Synoptics is future, but in John it is present. One judges oneself by whether or not one accepts Jesus. Jesus says that he "did not come to judge the world" (John 12:47), but nevertheless there is a judgment, and that judgment is one that one imposes upon oneself by one's attitude toward Jesus.

Not only does the idea of the Kingdom of God practically disappear from John's gospel, but the ethic of Jesus, which in the Synoptics demands right relationships with persons, disappears (See Mt. 25:31-46). All that is replaced in John with the rather general command, "If you love me, you will keep my commandments,"--but those commandments are never spelled out. This kind of reinterpretation is not what one would expect from an eyewitness.

The final problem with the idea that the Apostle John was the author is that there is a dual tradition about him. According to one tradition he lived to a ripe old age in Ephesus, dying at about the age of 95 or 100, the only apostle to die a natural death, his martyrdom being referred to as a white martyrdom because he did not die a martyr in the same way in which the other disciples did. There is a story of how as an aged man he was carried into the church meeting in Ephesus and they would ask him to speak and he would say "little children, love one another," and that's about all he could say, but they loved him for that. The problem with that tradition is that there is another tradition that he died very early--the second of the disciples to die. The only disciple whose death is recorded in the New Testament is James, the brother of John, and according to this second tradition John died very shortly after the death of his brother James. This tradition was discovered quite a number of years ago in the writings of Papias known as the DeBoor fragments. It is also supported by an ancient Calendar of Martyrs. Matthew 20:22 records a prediction by Jesus that James and John should die as martyrs and the recording of that prediction is presumptive evidence that it was fulfilled. One does not remember predictions that are not fulfilled. When there are contradictory traditions, how does one decide which one is right? It just cannot be possible that both are true. John could not have been martyred, the second disciple to die, and at the same time have lived to a ripe old age and die a natural death at Ephesus. When one has to choose between two contradictory traditions, one looks for a reason as to why one or the other could have been useful. What need was it created, or developed, to meet? If you need to have the gospel of John written by an apostle, that would seem to be a reason to create the tradition that he lived a long, long time. Not all scholars will agree to that. Some will, but others think that John the Apostle may somehow be associated with the community that produced the Gospel, but almost none think that he wrote it as it now stands.

So the Fourth Gospel, as the present writer understands it, comes out of a community; it is not directly dependent upon the writings or the memory of John the Apostle, although he may be in the early history of that community.

If the Apostle John did not write this gospel, who did?

One view holds that the gospel was written by an unknown Greek-thinking, Greek-speaking Christian who sought to reinterpret Jesus for the Greek mind. The Gospel uses a Greek style of writing, with dialogue and an appreciation for the precise meaning of Greek words. John sometimes uses apparent synonyms, but he is very aware of the shades of difference in meaning between the words;[4] he uses the concept of the Logos which belonged to the Stoics and to Philo, the Jewish scholar of Alexandria, who used the term in interpreting Judaism for the Greeks; he uses the Greek concept of eternal life. There is a lot to suggest that this writer was seeking to--among many other things--at least interpret Jesus for the Greek mind.

A new concept that is widely followed now is that the gospel comes out of a Jewish Christian community that was in conflict with the orthodox synagogue of its town. According to this view, this Jewish Christian group had originally had a very good relationship with the synagogue and many of its members probably worshiped in the synagogue on Saturday and in the Jewish Christian church on Sunday. But Judaism became concerned about Christianity and introduced into its service, sometime about 80 A. D., a prayer known as the Birkath ha-Minim or the Twelfth Benediction. An ancient fragment giving this benediction has been found, so we are no longer dependent upon material that came down through the Middle Ages when the conflict between the Jews and the Christians was so terribly intense that a lot of material got changed. The benediction went something like this:

For the apostates let there be no hope [apostates being people
that fall away from the faith] and let the arrogant government
be speedily uprooted on our days. [The arrogant government
would, of course, be Rome.] Let the Nazarenes [the
Christians] and the Minim [heretics] be destroyed in a
moment, and let them be blotted out of the Book of Life and
not be inscribed together with the righteous. Blessed art thou,
O Lord who humblest the proud![5]

Now imagine yourself a first-century Jewish Christian, attending a
synagogue service and this benediction was being said, and you were
expected to say it along with the others: you couldn't say it because you
would be pronouncing a curse upon yourself. If a person was seen stumbling
or halting when they said this benediction, they were called up before the
Ark and had to say it solo. You have been a follower of Jesus, but you have
also been staying in the synagogue and this benediction was suddenly
introduced. You are expelled! and you are angry about it. In such a
situation, the relationships between the synagogue and the Christian group
would become very, very tense. If one looks at the ninth chapter of John, one
finds a dialogue in which a man is healed from blindness and his parents are
asked to testify and they refuse because the Jews have determined that
anybody who recognizes Jesus as Messiah will be excommunicated from the
synagogue. In the time of Jesus nobody was excommunicated from the
synagogue for following him, but that passage reflects what was taking place
in the period from 85 to 95 or thereabouts.

Another thing in John that makes it appear that it might come out of a
community in which there was this kind of conflict is that the enemies of
Jesus are simply "the Jews." There is no recognition that Jesus was a Jew, no
recognition that the twelve disciples were Jews, no recognition as in the
Synoptics that the enemies of Jesus were particular groups, like the Scribes
and the Pharisees. The enemies are just "the Jews."

Such a Jewish Christian community, in spite of its conflict with the
synagogue, would still reflect its Jewish background in its writings. It has
already been suggested that the idea of the Logos may have had its roots in
the Old Testament. John can also be seen as a midrash. Midrash was a
typical Jewish way of writing. In the Old Testament I and II Chronicles is a
re-writing of Kings to make it apply to a much later date in history. Midrash

was a way of taking scripture and reinterpreting it quite freely to make it apply to a new situation and a new time. Midrash tended to use certain literary structures. It tended to use a chiastic structure; i.e., a structure with line a, line b, line c. The next line would be c-1 and it would parallel line c in thought, the next line would be b-1, paralleling line b; and the next line would be a-1, paralleling line a. This paralleling may run not only to "c," but halfway down the alphabet. Chiastic structure is a rather typical Old Testament form and it is found in John in many places, including the prologue.

Figure 1.   Chiastic Structure.

a a^1

b b^1

c

Note: The sequence moves down the first column and up the second.

This structure may be found in a single paragraph, as in the illustration below from John 6:36-40, or in a larger pattern, as is the case with the illustration from the Signs.

Figure 2. Two Illustrations of Chiastic Structure.

Chiasm as found in John 6:36-40[6]

a. 36: seeing and not believing a^1. 40: looking and believing

b. 37: not driving out what the b^1. 39: losing nothing of what
   Father has given   He has given

c. 38: I have come down from heaven

The Chiastic Pattern of the Signs[7]

a. The Wedding at Cana (2:1-12) a^1. The *blood & water*
   [wine (=blood) & water]   from Jesus' side

b. The restoration of the *dying* b^1. Resurrection of
   son (4:46-54)   *dead* Lazarus (11:1-41)

c. *Sabbath healing* at c^1. *Sabbath healing*
   Bethesda (5:1-16)   of blind man (9:1-41)

d. The Feeding of the Multitude (6:1-71)

Another typical Jewish form of writing was called *inclusio*. In the story of creation in Genesis 2, man is created first, then everything else is created, then woman is created--and some people say "Aha, that shows women at the bottom, they are the last and the least!" Anybody who says that does not understand the Jewish way of writing. To put something at the beginning and to put something at the end indicated that both are equal. They form a circle that includes the whole: *inclusio*. John has *inclusio* after *inclusio* after *inclusio*. So, very probably, this Gospel comes out of a Jewish Christian community in conflict with its neighboring orthodox synagogue.

Finally, in terms of how the gospel may have come, John may be the gospel of a Hellenistic (that is, Greek) Jewish Christian community. This concept recognizes the elements of truth in both the idea that the gospel is Greek in background and that it is Jewish in background. Before Christianity there were large Greek Jewish or (Hellenistic Jewish) communities that were in tension with Palestinian Judaism. These were Jews who lived out in the larger Greek or Roman world and who were more liberal in their religion than were their fellow Palestinian Jews. There was enough tension between them so that they had their own synagogues in Jerusalem. They would come up to Jerusalem for the Temple, but the tension was so great that they wanted their own synagogues, and Christianity first appealed to those Hellenistic Jews. Stephen, the first Christian martyr was a Hellenistic Jew. The first "deacons" that were chosen in the organization of the church in the Book of Acts all have Greek names, and one of them is specifically referred to as a proselyte--that is, a person who was originally a Gentile who had converted to Judaism. These Hellenistic Jews played a major part in the beginnings of Christianity and in the spread of Christianity, being the first to take it outside of Palestine, taking it up to Antioch, according to Acts.

According to this view the Johannine church was of Hellenistic Jewish background. It was in tension with orthodox Judaism and it was also in tension with what Raymond Brown calls the apostolic churches. The apostolic churches were those that looked to Peter as the source of authority, and the Johannine community is one that says authority in the church belongs to the beloved disciple. This is why one of the later chapters in this book deals with the tension between the beloved disciple and Peter. Brown in his book, *The Community of the Beloved Disciple*, develops the idea that there were several different churches with different concepts of church authority and organization and so on. The church which was to eventually become the "mainline" church he calls the apostolic church. The Johannine church was in opposition to this in terms of where it found authority and also in terms of its understanding of Jesus as Christ.[8] Furthermore, the gospel seems to be the product of a group of writers, a school, a Johannine School, if you will. It produced a midrash on Matthew, Mark and Luke to support its understanding of Jesus, of his message and of the authority of the Spirit in the churches. This school, however, had one dominate figure--the gospel as it now stands is clearly not the work of a committee! For want of a better term, this dominate person will sometimes be called "the Evangelist," and sometimes "John," but with no suggestion that he was the disciple by that name.

10

Chapter I Endnotes

1.   Maynard, Arthur H., "The Function of Apparent Synonyms and Ambiguous Words in the Fourth Gospel," *Abstracts of Dissertations*, University Chronicles Series, (University of Southern California Press, Los Angeles, 1950), 210-211.

2.   3:3, 5; 18:36.

3.   The references to the resurrection "at the last day" in chapter 6 are probably to be regarded as later additions, but in any event the whole emphasis of that chapter is on possessing eternal life in the present world.

4.   Maynard, loc. cit.

5.   Martyn, J. Louise, *History and Theology in the Fourth Gospel*, revised ed. (Nashville: Abingdon, 1979), 58.

6.   This illustration is based on Raymond E. Brown, S.S., *The Gospel According to John I-XII* (The Anchor Bible, N. Y.: Doubleday & Co., 1966) 275-276, who credits it to the work of Léon-Dufour.

7.   This structure was called to my attention by Professor Joseph A. Grassi in a paper, "The Role of Jesus' Mother in John's Gospel" (*Catholic Biblical Quarterly*, Jan. 1986). Grassi attributes it to the work of M. Girard. "La composition structurelle des sept signs dans le quartrième évangile," SR 9 (1980) 315-324. The blood and water at the cross is not usually counted in a list of Johannine signs, but the chiastic structure makes a good argument for including it.

8.   Brown, Raymond E., S.S., *The Community of the Beloved Disciple* (N. Y.: Paulist Press, 1979).

Chapter II

Jesus, the Divine Being

In the last chapter it was noted that the Jesus of the Fourth Gospel is no longer a Jewish Messianic King, but that he is a pre-existent, divine Logos. This pre-existent Logos becomes flesh, enters into the world, comes to the time of his ministry, and then is "glorified," i.e., taken back to the Father. The descent of the Spirit at the time of the baptism does not in some way establish a unique relationship between Jesus and God, as it clearly does in Mark, but it rather is only a sign to John the Baptist, so that he may testify that this is the one who was before him. Jesus, as "the divine Only Son, who leans upon his Father's breast," (Jn. 1:18, Goodspeed) has always been in a unique relationship with God.[1]

Johannine commentators generally point out that the term *logos* (word) is used in the Prologue in an exalted and metaphysical sense which nowhere reappears in the body of the Gospel,[2] and therefore dismiss the concept of a pre-existent Logos based on the Prologue as foreign to the Gospel as a whole. The evidence that the Prologue is an earlier hymn that has been adapted by the Evangelist has lent support to the view that the Logos concept does not reappear in the gospel, but this does not necessarily follow, for as Howard has well said, "The Prologue as it stands is now an integral part of the Gospel."[3] While it is true that the Logos is personified only in the Prologue, the term appears in some thirty-five verses scattered throughout the Gospel. A study of these passages indicates that the Greek *logos* is used with a wide range of meaning, but that the tendency is to use it to indicate "the word" not just as a statement, or not even as the total message of Jesus, but to use it with the connotation of "the revelation of God," or to indicate the spiritual relationship between Jesus and God.[4] *Logos* appears four times in the great prayer of chapter 17, in passages which well illustrate its significance.

The first passage is verses 6-8, which involves both the term *logos* and its apparent synonym, *hrēma*:

> I have manifested thy name to the men whom thou gavest me out of the world; . . . and they have kept thy word (*logos*). Now they know that everything that thou hast given me is from thee; for I have given them the words *hrēma* which thou didst send me.

The distinction between *logos* and *hrēma* cannot be between the divine word and mere human sayings, for both are from God. Nor can the distinction be between the total message of Christ and detached utterances, for the Evangelist is not suggesting that Christ has held back, but rather that he has passed on that which God has given. The words take on significance when one thinks of *logos* as standing for the *total* revelation, including the person and works, as well as the words of Jesus. The passage might be paraphrased: I have manifested thy name to those you gave me. . .and they have been true to the revelation. They know everything for I have given them the teachings you sent me.

In verses 14 and 17 the term *logos* might also be translated "revelation." It is this "revelation" that has caused the world to hate the disciples because it has separated them from the world. Obviously it is something which partakes of the divine that has caused such a separation. At verse 17 this "word" or "revelation" is described as truth.

At first glance such a translation does not seem appropriate in verse 20, where Jesus prays: "I do not pray for these only, but also for those who are to believe on me through their *word*." Yet when one reads further, and notes that Jesus prays that the disciples may be brought into perfect unity with God, and when one remembers that he has just prayed that they may be sanctified even as he sanctifies himself, it is not unreasonable to believe that the Evangelist is here saying that the disciples, and probably by implication the church of his own day, have been entrusted by Jesus not with mere words, but with the whole revelation.

This relationship of the "words" of Jesus to the pre-existent Logos concept has been stressed by Scott, who maintains that the Evangelist considers the words of Jesus to be the crowning proof of his divinity and to possess a direct power and efficacy. Little of ethical teaching or spiritual illumination is said, the words being assertions, in various forms, of the divine nature and life-giving purpose of Jesus. Scott well says:

> ...The word of God which had become incarnate in Him found utterance through His words, and they had therefore a mysterious value and efficacy. The divine nature imparted itself by means of them. They passed into the hearts of those who would receive them like the very breath of God, and were found to be spirit and life.[5]

By using the term *logos* not only in the Prologue, but throughout the gospel, the Evangelist is seeking to show his readers that Jesus is a divine being.[6]

Nowhere is this Johannine concept of Jesus as a divine being more clearly seen than in the account of the first public act of Jesus, the changing of the water to wine at Cana of Galilee. The mother of Jesus brings to him the report that the wine is gone, and he answers, "Woman, what have I to do with thee?" (Jn. 2:4, King James). This statement is a translation of a rather uncommon Greek idiomatic expression which literally means "what to me and to you." The expression is found four times in the Septuagint, five times elsewhere in the Gospels, and four times in the apocryphal *Acts of Thomas.* A study of these passages indicates that this idiom is everywhere used to indicate that the two parties have nothing in common with each other. It is further significant that every synoptic use of this idiom involves the recognition of the divine nature of Jesus by demons or by persons possessed by demons. Many commentators and translators have felt that this statement was unduly harsh, representing an attitude toward his mother out of harmony with the spirit of Jesus, and have tried to soften its force, but the usage of this idiom elsewhere makes it very clear that it is the intent of the Johannine writer to have Jesus indicate a complete separation between himself and his mother. He is in effect saying, "Woman, you and I have nothing in common with each other."

Because this statement is followed by the statement "Mine hour is not yet come," many commentators suggest that Jesus is saying to his mother, "Do not try to direct me, It is not yet time for me to act" (Jn. 2:4, Goodspeed). Such an interpretation, however, is rendered utterly meaningless by the fact that Jesus does proceed to act at once on the suggestion of his mother and demonstrates his power by performing his first miracle. A statement that it is not time for him to act is contradictory to the situation.

Help in understanding this passage comes when one notes that the identical expression, except for a change of a pronoun to the plural, is found in Mark's gospel immediately before the first miracle. The relationship between Mark and John at this point is striking. In both the order has been (a) the witness of John the Baptist, (b) the calling of the disciples, (c) the first miracle, in the account of which this idiom is used. John has preceded these three events by his prologue, which is easily explained by the more polished literary character of his work, while Mark has inserted the temptation experience between the baptism and the calling of the disciples. The omission of this item by John is explained by his exalted concept of the divine nature of Jesus. He is a person who is above the possibility of temptation.

In Mark this idiom, "What have you to do with us" (Mk. 1:24), is uttered by demons, as is true of every other synoptic use of it (Mk. 8:29, Lk. 4:34; Mk. 5:7; Mt. 8:29), and is a recognition by a higher than human order of beings of the divinity of Jesus. It seems most probable that John, in compiling his material, found this recognition of the higher nature of Jesus in his sources,[7] a recognition that was in harmony with his own interpretation of Jesus. But the Fourth Evangelist could not have this recognition come from demons, not only because Jesus does not cast out demons in this gospel,[8] but also because in this gospel it is part of the function of Jesus to reveal his divine nature. He was, furthermore, confronted with the historical fact of a misunderstanding between Jesus and his family (Mk. 3:31-35). By having Jesus indicate his divine nature to his mother with the words "what to me and to you," he is true to his sources and at the same time explains the gulf which separated Jesus from his family. When Jesus says to his mother "We have nothing in common!" he is indicating that he is no longer the son of Mary, but that he is now moving on a divine level where he has no filial relationship to her. Having made that break with his mother, and having asserted his divine nature, he can then demonstrate that nature by performing his miracle, which, in John's gospel, is a "sign" of his divinity.

This interpretation of this passage is strengthened by the addition of the words, "My hour has not yet come." This expression is an invitation to the reader to look to that point at which Jesus' hour has come. The *hour* comes in the Fourth Gospel with the glorification of Jesus (Jn. 17:1-20:29). While strictly "glorification" is the return to the Father, for the Evangelist all those events connected with the return--crucifixion, resurrection, and ascension (not mentioned as such in John)--are telescoped into the "glorification." And when one looks at that event, the mother of Jesus (who is never called "Mary" in this gospel) is there, and the relationship which Jesus has disavowed at the beginning of his ministry is reestablished with the Beloved Disciple taking the place of Jesus, by the words, "Behold, your mother!" (Jn. 19:27).

There are three levels of life for Jesus in the Fourth Gospel. There is Jesus, the son of Mary, whose very existence has been de-emphasized by the omission of the birth narratives and of her name. With "O woman, what have you to do with me? My hour has not yet come" (Jn. 2:4), Jesus terminates this level and moves on to the plane of the divine revelation in history. This level terminates with the glorification, which represents his pre-incarnate state at one with God.

Figure 3

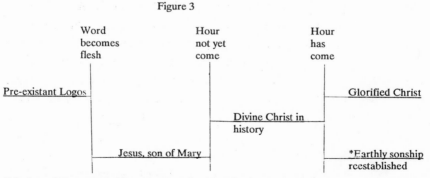

*Mother of Jesus probably represents the Church, the Body of Christ on earth, and the "Beloved Disciple" represents any church leader who is in the bosom of Christ as Christ is in the bosom of God.

As a divine being moving through history on the plane of the divine revelation, the Christ of the Fourth Gospel is far less human than the Jesus of the Synoptics. At first glance the display of emotion attributed to Jesus at the death of Lazarus would seem to deny this statement. Here in the short space of three verses Jesus is said to be "moved with indignation in the spirit," to be "troubled," and to have "wept," but on closer examination it becomes apparent that the emotions here are not the emotions of a human, but of a divine being. The word which the Greek uses for the statement that he was "moved with indignation" is *embrimaomai*, a word which in its root means "to snort like a horse," but elsewhere when John wants to speak of the anger of persons, he uses *cholaō*, a word meaning "to be full of bile." *Embrimaomai* was used in the Old Testament (Lam. 2:6) for the anger of God, and it seems likely that the writer has deliberately chosen a word used in the Greek Old Testament for the anger of God rather than the word which he had previously used for the anger of human beings. The statement that Jesus was "troubled," literally reads "he troubled himself." Westcott, one of the older commentators on this gospel, but a man who often had a keen discernment for the Johannine use of words, suggests that the passive form here indicates that Jesus has voluntarily taken to himself the emotional feelings which come to others involuntarily.[9]

Not only is the anger of Jesus different from the anger of human beings, but his weeping, also, is different. *Klaiō* which means "to wail," is used in 11:31, 33 of the weeping of Mary and of the Jews, but when the Evangelist speaks of the weeping of Jesus, the verb changes to *dakruō*, which means "to shed tears." Elsewhere throughout the gospel, whether it be to predict the weeping of the disciples in 16:20, or to tell of the weeping of Mary at the tomb (20:11, 13, 15), the word *klaiō* is used, and in fact, *dakruō* does not appear elsewhere in the New Testament. The very choice of words suggests that Jesus, though he weeps, is angry and disquieted, is still very much the Christ, the Son of God.

Another way that John has used to indicate the divinity of Jesus is found in the formula, *ego eimi*. Literally this means "I am," but the "I" is emphasized by the use of the pronoun, since the form of the verb made the use of the pronoun unnecessary unless stress was desired. Bernard has shown that in both the Greek Old Testament and in the pre-Christian writings of the Egyptian mystery religions, this phrase was used to indicate the speaking of deity.[10] A study of its twenty-two appearances in the Gospel of John reveals that when it is used absolutely, or with a predicate of messianic implications, it means not simply "I am," but rather, "I, the Christ, am." Furthermore, whenever Jesus uses the phrase in the Fourth Gospel, it is always used either absolutely, or with a predicate of messianic character.[11] The formula first appears in 4:26, where Jesus makes his divine nature known to the Samaritan woman in the statement "I (*egō eimi*) who speak to you am he." It next appears in the account of the storm at sea, where Jesus says, "*Egō eimi*, do not be afraid." This is not just self-identification, but must mean, "It is I, the Christ, the one who brings spiritual peace." The phrase appears in all of the "I am" statements of this gospel: "I am the bread of life" (Jn. 6:35), "I am the light of the world" (Jn. 8:12), "I am the door" (Jn. 10:7), etc. These are all statements of the divine nature of Christ. Space does not permit the mentioning of every use of this formula, but there are two that are too interesting to let pass. One is in 13:19, where Jesus makes the statement "I tell you this now, before it takes place, that when it does take place you may believe that I am (*egō eimi*)." Here is divinity not only implied by the absence of any predicate, expressed or implied, but also by the fact that Jesus has assumed the divine prerogative of foretelling the future.[12] The other usage is at 18:5, where Judas and the officers have come to arrest Jesus. In reply to the question, "Whom do you seek?" they answer, "Jesus of Nazareth," whereupon Jesus says "*egō eimi* (I am he)." It can, and indeed has been argued, that this is simply an identification, but not only is the implied predicate, "Jesus of Nazareth," who in this gospel is always a divine being, but also, the effect of this statement on the arresting party is that "they went backward and fell to the ground." Rather obviously their reaction implies that the phrase *egō eimi* has revealed to them that they are in the presence of the divine.

Yet another indication of the divine nature of Jesus in the Fourth Gospel is his sense of union with the Father. In the Synoptics Jesus talks of "*Our* Father," as in the Lord's prayer, or of "*Your* Father," as in the Sermon on the Mount, but in John these pronouns are replaced with "*My* Father." The

Fatherhood of God is no longer a concept which expresses the relationship of the individual believer to God but is reserved for the special relationship of Jesus to God. Repeatedly he speaks of himself as the revelation of the Father--"No one has ever seen God; the only Son, who is in the bosom of the Father, he has made him known" (Jn. 1:18); ". . . if you knew me, you would know my Father also" (Jn. 8:19); or of his union with the Father--"Jesus, knowing. . . that he had come from God and was going to God" (Jn. 13:3); ". . . he who has seen me has seen the Father" (Jn. 14:9); "I am in the Father and the Father in me" (Jn. 14:10).

Additional evidence that Jesus is a divine being as he moves through the pages of the Fourth Gospel is found in the series of six signs which replace the miracles of the Synoptics. In the Synoptics the miracles are, almost without exception, done to meet human need, and are preceded by an evidence of faith on the part of the person helped. In John they are signs to show the glory of God, and to help the people believe.

The first of these signs is the turning of water into wine. This miracle is unlike any found in the Synoptics, but it may nevertheless be closely related to the synoptic tradition. In that tradition Jesus had identified his teaching with "new wine." "No one puts new wine into old wineskins" (Mk. 2:22). Further, it seems especially significant that this remark in Mark comes immediately following a statement by Jesus about a wedding--"Can the wedding guests fast while the bridegroom is with them?" This sign is a dramatic presentation of the same truth. The six water pots were for use "for the Jewish rites of purification." This tasteless, insipid, lifeless water is changed by the presence of Jesus to life-giving, sparkling wine. (This isn't good material for a temperance sermon, but it correctly reflects the popular attitude of the day, caused in part by the fact that water often came from stagnant cisterns, and was almost certain, whatever its source, to be contaminated.) The symbolism of the miracle is that here is one who has given a spiritual quality to religion, while the miracle itself serves as a sign which "manifested his glory" and caused "his disciples to believe on him."

Norman A. Huffman, Professor Emeritus of Religion at Willamette University, has suggested that this "sign" may also reflect the sacramental interests of the Evangelist, the wine of the Eucharist replacing the water of purification as a mode of salvation. This suggestion is very plausible, as John reflects a definite sacramental interest in his treatment of the Feeding of the Five Thousand.[13] Ultimately, however, he is not a sacramentarian, but is interested in the spiritual realities of religion. See Jn. 6:63.

The second sign is the healing of the nobleman's son (Jn. 4:46-54) by "remote control." While there are some differences between this story and the healing of the centurion's servant in the Synoptics (Mt. 8:5ff.; Lk. 7:6ff.), there are enough similarities to make it probable that this is the Johannine version of that incident. Both put the residence of the sick person at Capernaum and make the healing telepathic. The outstanding difference between the Synoptic and the Johannine accounts is that in Matthew and Luke the patient is the servant while in John he is the son. Both Matthew and Luke use for "servant" the Greek word *pais*, which could mean either, although Luke makes it clear that he intends it to mean servant by also using the word *doulos*. John seems to have picked up the word *pais*, which he used in verse 51, and then taking its other meaning, to have preferred the word *huios*, which means "son."[14] Bernard makes much out of the fact that the story as it stands is not a record of a "miracle." Jesus simply hears the description of the son's illness, and says "Go; your son will live." Many a physician, says Bernard, on hearing the description of a disease, can predict whether or not it will end fatally.[15] But this seems to be a modernizing of the story. Bernard himself admits that in the time of John such foreknowledge would have been regarded as superhuman, and the fact that the servants report that the son began to convalesce at the hour Jesus spoke the words seems specifically to imply that it was a miracle of telepathic healing. The gospel writer is saying that this man who brings new spiritual life into the old forms of religion also can bring new life into a sick boy at some distance--he is a divine being.

The third Johannine sign is the healing of the impotent man (Jn. 5:2-9). Whereas the first two were clearly labeled "signs," this one is not so called. It seems to have two purposes in the developments which follow. First, it causes difficulty with the Jews because it represented work on the sabbath, so that the Jews start to persecute Jesus and seek to slay him. Secondly, it becomes an opportunity for Jesus to indicate his relationship with God. In the Synoptics his usual answer to the charge of sabbath-breaking is to show, as in Mark 2:25, that there is Old Testament precedent for overriding strict observance of the law in case of necessity, or to appeal to the legality of doing good on the sabbath (Mk. 3:4). In Mark 2:28 Jesus laid down the principle that "the Son of man is lord even of the sabbath." The phrase "Son of man" is ambiguous. It can mean "human being," in which case Jesus is restating the idea that the sabbath was made for man and not man for the sabbath, or it can be a synonym for "messiah," in which case Jesus is appealing to his divine prerogative as his authority for sabbath-breaking. John follows this last line of reasoning by having Jesus say, "My Father is working still, and I am working." This identification of himself with God promptly results in a charge of blasphemy being made against him by the Jews, but that charge is ignored and Jesus goes on to comment on his divine role. In short, the purpose of this miracle seems to be to afford Jesus an opportunity to reveal his identity with the Father.

At first glance this miracle seems to be unrelated to anything in the Synoptics, but in Mark 2:1-12 there is a story of Jesus healing a man sick with the palsy, in which he uses almost the identical phrase which he uses in healing the man by the pool. In Mark he says to the man, "rise, take up your pallet, and walk," and the word for "pallet" (*krabattos*) is the same in both John and Mark and is not used elsewhere in the New Testament except at Mark 6:55 and Acts 5:15; 9:33. Furthermore this healing in Mark results in a charge of blasphemy being leveled against Jesus. John's account says nothing about the forgiving of sins, but it is implied in the charge which Jesus gives to the man, "Sin no more, that nothing worse befall you."

Further, if one looks at the end of the second chapter of Mark, one finds a charge of sabbath-breaking made against Jesus because he had plucked grain on the sabbath. It is here that Jesus answers with what may be interpreted as an appeal to his authority as son of man, discussed above. There are many differences between this Markan material and the Johannine sign. The Markan incidents take place in Capernaum, the Johannine in Jerusalem. Those who seek to destroy him for sabbath-breaking are Pharisees who take counsel with the Herodians in Mark (3:6), while they are Jerusalem Jews in John. In John the charge of sabbath-breaking and of blasphemy both come out of one incident, in Mark they come out of three incidents (there is a second charge of sabbath-breaking in Mark 3:1-6). Nevertheless, there are some striking similarities. (1) The healing is marked by the identical formula on the lips of Jesus. (2) The incidents result in the charges of blasphemy and sabbath-breaking. (3) Jesus makes his final appeal to his divine nature, although in characteristic Johannine fashion the messianic "Son of man" is replaced with a long discourse about the union between Jesus and God. (4) Finally, in both, the hostility created by the situation causes Jesus to leave the scene of his activity--in Mark he goes to the region of Tyre and Sidon, and in John he leaves Jerusalem for Galilee. Are the similarities between the two great enough to support the theory that John has created his third sign from this Markan material? If not, how can one account for the similarities between the two passages? Certainly if Mark is the source of the third sign, John has been very free in the way in which he used his source.[16]

Whatever one may conclude about the source of the third sign, there can be no doubt about its purpose--it is used by the Evangelist to give Jesus an opportunity to enter into a thoroughly Greek discourse about his union with the Father. This is the divine being moving across the pages of history.

The fourth sign is the feeding of the five thousand (Jn. 6:4-13). This miracle is adopted with but slight changes from the synoptic parallels (Mt. 14:13ff.; Lk. 9:11ff.; Mk. 6:33ff.). The slight changes that are made are in the direction of making the account suggest a eucharistic meal. Thus while the Synoptics used the word *eulogein* for the blessing of the bread, John changes that to *euxaristein*,[17] a word which early came to be used in a special sense in connection with the Holy Communion. Whereas the disciples help Jesus distribute the bread in the Synoptics, in John he gives it directly to the people (the words translated in the King James "to the disciples, and the disciple" [v.11] are not in the best manuscripts). That which is left is collected in both the Synoptics and in John, but in the Synoptics it seems to be collected to show the abundance of the miracle, while in John it is collected for the sacerdotal reason, "that nothing be lost." The institution of the Last Supper is not mentioned as such in the Fourth Gospel, and this "sign" takes its place, giving the writer an opportunity to introduce the long discourse centering around the statement, "I am the bread of life." But this sign not only permits Jesus to further reveal his nature by setting the stage for this teaching discourse, but it causes the men who see it to testify, "This is indeed *the* prophet who is to come into the world!" (Jn. 6:14). This testimony does not express the true nature of Jesus, but at least the people comprehend something of his divinity.[18]

The calming of the storm on the lake (Jn. 6:16-21) is not called either a "sign" or a "work" by John, and is not included in many lists of the "signs" of the Fourth Gospel, but the healing of the impotent man is likewise not designated as a "sign" by the Evangelist,[19] and as good a case can be made for including the one as the other in a consideration of the "signs" in this gospel. Again John has followed his synoptic sources, this time rather condensing the account. Bernard, and some others, have laid hold on the fact that the Greek of John's account can be literally translated "They saw Jesus walking *by* the sea" instead of "*on* the sea," and have denied that there is a miracle implied. The force of the whole paragraph, however, seems to be otherwise. It opens with a double emphasis on the fact that it was dark. "When evening came, his disciples went down to the sea, . . . It was now dark, and Jesus had not yet come to them" (Jn. 6:16f.). This double emphasis is not found in either of the synoptic accounts of this miracle, and John is too good a writer to add it unless it has significance. The force of this passage is undoubtedly to be found in an allegorical interpretation. As Quimby suggests, "The storm-tossed disciples were, like Nicodemus, in the dark without Christ. To be in the dark without Christ is to dwell in terrible danger!"[20] When Jesus reached the boat, the danger was over. Strachan makes a very probable suggestion when he says that this passage may have been intended to symbolize to the Church of John's day the spiritual presence of Christ amid the storms of life.[21] The fact that Jesus calms the disciples (nothing is said about the calming of the *sea*, unless it is implied in the fact that the ship came immediately to land) with the words *egō eimi*,[22] suggests that so far as John is concerned the important thing here is that Jesus is a divine being who can come through any storm and bring peace to his disciples.

The next sign is the healing of the man born blind (Jn. 9:1-41). This has been specifically labeled by the Evangelist as a sign, the Pharisees asking, "how can a man who is a sinner do such signs?" (Jn. 9:16). Its purpose, like the others, is to give Jesus an opportunity to manifest his divine nature. Some of the Pharisees admit that he may be *a* prophet (not *the* prophet of 6:14), but the healed blind man is excommunicated from the synagogue when he confesses that Jesus must be from God. Jesus then reveals himself as the Son of man and condemns the Pharisees for their spiritual blindness.

For John this sign is much more than a mere healing, or even than a demonstration of the divine nature of Jesus. The blind man is a symbol of the Jews who were converted to Christianity. His experience with the synagogue represents the unhappy but historically accurate experience of the Jewish Christians. But despite his rejection by his people (i.e., his parents) and his synagogue, he has the gift of spiritual sight.[23]

This passage is very interesting in the way in which it reveals the style of the writer. The whole symbolism of the passage hinges on the ambiguity of *blepō*, one of the words for "seeing." In verses 7, 15, 19, and 25 *blepō* is used for physical seeing, but in verses 39 and 41 it is used to indicate the ability to comprehend spiritual realities. The reference is clearly to the Jewish leaders who think that they "see" but are really blind to spiritual things in that they do not accept Jesus, whereas the man formerly blind has "believed." The former are guilty of sin because they do not admit their spiritual blindness.[24]

But while the author has played upon the physical and spiritual connotations of *blepō*, three other Greek words for seeing, *ediō, theoreō,* and *horaō* are also found in this story. The passage opens with Jesus "seeing" (*ediō*) the blind man. This is the normal use of this verb. The next use of the verb "to see" is in verse 7, where the blind man washes and comes seeing (*blepō*). When in the next verse the Evangelist speaks of the neighbors who had seen (*theoreō*) the man before, the term suggests that they had been spectators to the fact, and it is the most appropriate word that could have been used.

Blepō continues to be used for the seeing of the blind man until verse 37, when Jesus replies to the blind man's request that he tell who the Son of

God is that he may believe by saying "You have seen (*horaō*) him, and it is he who speaks to you." Schaff comments on this passage saying, with Lücke, "The seeing really seems to contain also an allusion to his spiritual *receiving of sight*."[25] This observation is supported by the confession of faith on the part of the blind man which immediately follows, and is in keeping with the higher meaning of "seeing with spiritual insight" which *horaō* so often carries. There is clearly in this passage a definite awareness of the various shadings and overtones of the different words for seeing, and they are not used synonymously, but with an appreciation for the subtle distinctions between them. While the whole symbolism of the passage depends on the double meaning of *blepō*, the author makes sure that the symbolism will not be missed by shifting to the word which he reserves for seeing with spiritual insight when he comes to the climax.[26]

The last sign, sixth or seventh, depending on whether or not the walking on the sea is counted, is the raising of Lazarus (Jn. 11:1-44). This sign, which is referred to as such by the Evangelist (Jn. 14:47), is appropriately the last, for it was the greatest of signs--the returning of one from the dead. There is no sign which this divine being cannot do.

The teaching dialogue which follows this sign will be discussed further in the next chapter, but it is interesting to note that this sign, like the others, seems to have its roots in the synoptic tradition. True, there is in the Synoptics no raising of Lazarus, which raises a serious question about the historicity of this incident, if it really happened, why do none of the Synoptics know this greatest of all miracles attributed to Jesus? But there is a parable about a man named Lazarus who dies and goes to "the bosom of Abraham" (Lk. 16:19-31). A certain rich Jew who has also died but has gone to Hades requests Father Abraham to send Lazarus back to warn his brothers so that they not suffer as he has. Father Abraham answers "If they will not listen to Moses and the prophets, they will not be convinced even if someone rises from the dead!" Further, Luke, rather close to the Lazarus parable, knows two women, Mary and Martha, who have exactly the same role in Luke as they do in John. Mary is spiritually sensitive while Martha does not understand spiritual things (Lk. 10:38-42). Also in Matthew and Mark there is an anointing by a woman at Bethany--see John 12:1-8. When one turns to

John's gospel one finds that one--whose name is Lazarus--does return from the dead, and what happens? As Luke has already said, the Jews do not believe--rather, they plot to kill Jesus.

Wherever one looks in the Fourth Gospel, one sees a Divine Being walking across its pages. Whether it be in the prologue, in the Logos concept, at the Wedding of Cana at the opening of his ministry, in the emotions which he expresses, in the formula, *egō eimi*, by which he identifies himself, or in the signs which he performs, the Jesus of the Fourth Gospel is not essentially Jesus, son of Mary, but he is the one who is "in the bosom of the Father." The divine nature of Jesus is consistently expressed in terms that would be understandable to the Greek and Gentile mind, but the Evangelist has made every page contribute toward his ultimate purpose--that his readers may "believe that Jesus is the Christ, the Son of God" (Jn. 20:31b).

Chapter II Endnotes

1.   Davis argues that for John the baptism is the time of the Incarnation. Jesus of Nazareth existed before this as a human figure, but the Christ, or what I have referred to as the pre-existent Logos, entered into Jesus at this point, and from this time on he is a Divine Being. There is considerable cogency to this argument, but it is not convincing to me. Davis, Guy M., Jr., "The Humanity of Jesus in John," *Journal of Biblical Literature*. 70:105-112, June, 1951. *Cf.* Titus, Eric L., *The Message of the Fourth Gospel* (N.Y.: Abingdon, 1957), 33, where this same view is stated but not argued.

2.   Scott, E. F., *The Fourth Gospel, Its Purpose and Theology*, second edition; (Edinburgh: T. and T. Clark, 1908). 115. *Cf.* J. Estlin Carpenter, *The Johannine Writings* (N.Y.: Houghton Mifflin Company, 1927), 155; G. H. C. Macgregor, *The Gospel of John*, James Moffatt, editor, *The Moffatt New Testament Commentary* (N.Y.: Doubleday, Doran and Company, Inc., 1929), *ad loc. Cf.* Raymond E. Brown, *John I-XII*, 18-23. Brown further feels that the Prologue comes from the Johannine Community but is not from the Evangelist.

3.   Howard, W. F., *Christianity according to St. John* (Philadelphia: Westminster Press, 1946), 47.

4.   Exceptions to this are found at 6:30; 7:36, 40; 19:8,13; and 21:23. 4:37 is uncertain. It may be an allusion to Micah 6:17, in which case it could be read "revelation."

5.   Scott, *op. cit.*, 171-172. *Cf.* Carpenter, *op. cit.*, 334.

6.   The material dealing with the *logos* concept is condensed from Maynard, Arthur H., *The Function of Apparent Synonyms and Ambiguous Words in the Fourth Gospel*, 45-68.

7.   My contention is that the sources for the Gospel of John are the synoptic gospels, which John has developed in a midrashic fashion. I have developed this in a book manuscript which I hope will soon be published. However the matter of source is not important to the development here.

8.   Ernest Cadman Colwell has an interesting explanation for this in his *John Defends the Gospel* (Chicago: Willett, Clark and Company, 1936).

9.   Westcott, Brooke Foss, *The Gospel According to St. John, with Introduction and Notes* (London: John Murray, 1882), *ad loc.*

10.   Bernard, J. H., *A Critical and Exegetical Commentary on the Gospel according to St. John*, A. H. Neile, editor, 2 vols., *The International Critical Commentary* (Edinburgh: T. and T. Clark, 1928), cxvii-cxii.

11.   Maynard, *Function of Apparent Synonyms and Ambiguous Words*, 405-413.

12.   Bernard, *op. cit., ad loc.*

13.   Norman A. Huffman, Professor Emeritus of Religion at Wilamette University, in personal conversation.

14. Bernard, *op. cit., ad loc.*

15. *Ibid.*, clxxx.

16. There is evidence that the Evangelist was equally free in his treatment of the Old Testament. See Edwin D. Freed, *Old Testament Quotations in the Gospel of John.* (Supplements to Novum Testamentum, vol. XI. Leiden: E. J. Brill, 1965), and C. Goodwin, "How Did John Treat His Sources?" paper read at the Society of Biblical Literature and Exegesis, New York, Dec. 28, 1951.

17. Bernard argues, with some logic, that this shift is not significant, but in view of the eucharistic tone of the whole of chapter 6, it seems significant to this writer. This position is supported by my doctoral research on these passages. Maynard, *Function of Apparent Synonyms and Ambiguous Words,* 296ff.

18. "The Prophet" was expected prior to the Messiah. This idea seems to have been based on Deut. 18:15: ". . . God will raise up for you a prophet like me (Moses)." That this "prophet" was not the Messiah is clear from Jn. 7:41, and is also indicated by the choice of Greek verbs in the present passage. *Ibid.*, 134ff.

19. Some argue that the healing of the impotent man is called a sign at 6:2, but that verse is a general reference to signs, and comes at some distance (57 verses) from the healing story.

20. Quimby, Chester W., *John: The Universal Gospel.* (N.Y.: The Macmillan Co., 1947), 139.

21. R. C. Strachan, cited by Macgregor, *op. cit., ad loc.*

22. *Supra*, 17.

23. For a detailed discussion of the way this sign reflects the relationship between Jewish Christians and the synagogue, see Martyn, *op. cit.*

24. Maynard, *Function of Apparent Synonyms and Ambiguous Words,* 128f.

25. Lange, John Peter, *A Commentary on the Holy Scriptures, The Gospel According to John*, Philip Schaff, editor and revisor (N.Y.: Charles Scribner's sons, 1884), *ad loc.*

26. Maynard, *Function of Apparent Synonyms and Ambiguous Words,* 140f.

Chapter III

Conversations with the Spiritually Dull

In the opening chapter it was pointed out that John replaces the parables of the Synoptic Gospels with dialogues with the spiritually dull. One of the first such is the conversation with Nicodemus (Jn. 3:1-21). This opens with Nicodemus coming to Jesus with the statement that he is a teacher "come from God." Jesus responds, "Truly, truly, I say to you, unless one is born anew, he cannot see the kingdom of God." This statement is rather widely recognized as the Johannine form of Mark 10:15, "Truly, I say to you whoever does not receive the kingdom of God like a little child shall not enter it," but John has made some radical changes in it. Being "like a little child" has been replaced with being "born anew," and this change seems to have been deliberately made to provide the setting for the conversation which follows. The word which is translated "anew" is *anōthen*, a word which could mean "again" or "anew," but which could also mean "from above." The whole point of the ensuing dialogue hangs on the ambiguous meaning of this word. Nicodemus, who despite the fact that he is a teacher of Israel, does not understand spiritual things, takes the lower meaning, asking how it is possible for him to experience a physical rebirth. Jesus then replies with the statement: "Unless one is born of water and the Spirit, he cannot enter the kingdom of God." Jesus, by restating his original point, has made it clear that it is a spiritual birth of which he was first speaking, but Nicodemus was too dull in spiritual comprehension to understand.

Nicodemus is scolded for not understanding, and Jesus then launches into a long discourse in which he speaks of his witness being validated by the fact that he is descended from heaven, of his coming death, and of his role as one who brings eternal life rather than judgment to the world.

While Nicodemus may be one of the ones who "loved darkness rather than light" (Jn. 3:19) since he came to Jesus by night, and may be a symbol for the fact that the Jewish leaders rejected Jesus, one is left with the impression that he is a distinctly minor figure in the discourse, whose chief function is to give Jesus an opportunity to explain his teaching.

The next conversation in which Jesus participates is that with the Samaritan woman (Jn. 4:1-42). Jesus, weary with travel, sits by Jacob's *pēgē*-- a well in the true sense of the word, with flowing water in it, rather than a cistern. A Samaritan woman comes, and Jesus asks her for a drink. The woman questions why a Jew should ask a drink from a Samaritan, and Jesus answers, "If you knew the gift of God, and who it is that is saying to you 'Give me a drink,' you would have asked him, and he would have given you living water." Since the whole conversation thus far has been in terms of the physical, and since flowing water, such as came from a *pēgē* was commonly called "living water,"[1] the woman fails to understand that Jesus is thinking in spiritual terms, and this misunderstanding creates a teaching situation.

The woman, thinking in terms of the physical, says, "Sir, you have nothing to draw with, and the *cistern* (RSV: well) is deep, where do you get that living water? Are you greater than our father Jacob?" (Jn. 4:11-12a) In the usual translation the word "well" is carried into this conversation, but the Greek word changes to *phrear*, a word which had for its primary meaning, "an artificial well," and which by general usage referred to a cistern. Since a *pēgē* was the more desirable type of well, it seems significant that it can be used for Jacob's well up to the point where Jesus is made to mention the water of life, after which point *pēgē* can only refer to Jesus, and Jacob's well becomes a mere "pit" or "cistern." The choice of words is a very subtle and artistic means of strengthening the symbolism of Jesus as the source of the water of life. It may very well be that Jacob's *phrear* is a symbol for the Samaritan religion.

Jesus now makes it clear that the water that he gives is greater than the water of the well. One who drinks from Jesus does not thirst again. Undoubtedly the meaning here is that one who follows the forms of the Samaritan faith must come back to its rituals continually, but with Jesus there is a mystical relationship with the believer which gives eternal life.

The dull Samaritan woman still fails to understand, and thinks of all the weary trips to the well she can save if she has some magic water after the drinking of which she will not thirst. Jesus tells her to call her husband, and she reports that she has none. Jesus then mentions five husbands, and the fact that she is now living with one who is not her husband. This passage is usually interpreted as indicating the moral condition of the woman, but if the symbolism which has already been suggested is correct, it may have meant something far more to John. The Samaritan religion did not have the whole of the Jewish Bible, but only the five books of the law. These are symbolized by the five husbands. The man who is not her husband is a symbol for the fact that the Samaritan faith is not the true religion--living in adultery being a symbol for falling away from the true faith at least as early as the Old Testament prophet, Hosea.

The woman now gets a certain amount of spiritual insight, declaring that Jesus is *a* prophet. Since the Johannine Jesus is much more than a prophet, Jesus follows with a discourse on spiritual worship. The woman then makes reference to the coming of the Messiah, and Jesus identifies himself to her. The woman now goes to the city to tell her friends, leaving her "water pot" behind her. This little phrase has been regarded as an insignificant point remembered by an eyewitness, or as indicating the joy with which the woman went, but if the symbolism which has been suggested is correct, the water pot is another symbol of the lifeless water of the Samaritan religion, and the woman, having found the Christ, the well of living water, can leave it behind because she has no further use for it.

The woman of Samaria is much more of a real life character than was Nicodemus, but like him she is spiritually dull, and this dialogue, like the former, is built on the patter of the misunderstanding of an ambiguous statement, the ambiguity in this instance arising out of a symbol, "living water," used with a spiritual interpretation.

Within the larger dialogue between Jesus and the Samaritan woman there is a side dialogue with another group of the spiritually dull, the disciples, and it, too, is dependent upon a play on words. The disciples, in John 4:8, have gone into the village to buy *trophē*, or food. They return, in verse 32, to hear Jesus say that he has food (*brōsis*) to eat that they know not of. The disciples think in terms of physical food, which the word could mean, but the writer has refrained from using it with that connotation. The disciples do not use *brōsis*, but simply ask if any man has brought him anything to eat. Jesus then answers, "My food (*brōma*, a variant form of *brōsis*) is to do the will of him who sent me." He then goes on to challenge them with the fact that the fields are ripe for harvest. Jesus is here calling the disciples to a successful mission in Samaria, such as the early church experienced, but his opportunity for this call has been furnished by the necessity to comment upon a statement which his spiritually-dull disciples have misunderstood.

Yet another conversation between Jesus and the spiritually dull is found in chapter six, where the Master discusses the feeding of the previous day with the multitude. Jesus opens the conversation with a statement in which he depreciates their spiritual comprehension: "Truly, truly, I say to you, You seek me, not because you saw signs, but because you *ate of the loaves, and were stuffed like animals (chortazō)*" (Jn. 6:26).[2] He then urges them to "not labor for the food (*brōsis*) which perishes (as the manna did), but for the food (*brōsis*) which endures to eternal life." The multitude now ask for a sign, pointing out that their fathers had eaten manna, which was "bread (*artos*) from heaven." Jesus answers that this bread was not given by Moses, but by "my Father," and comments that "the bread of God is that which comes down from heaven, and gives life to the world." In words which remind one of the Samaritan woman's request for water, they ask for "this bread." Jesus then, as with the woman, identifies himself, this time as "the bread of life" come down from heaven to do the will of the Father and to give eternal life to those who believe.

In addition to the similarity between the multitude's request for "bread" and the Samaritan woman's request for water, there are other interesting parallels between these two discourses. Just as *pēgē* can be used of Jacob's well until Jesus reveals himself as the source of living water, *artos* can be used of material bread until Jesus reveals himself as the bread of life, after which *artos* is used only with the spiritual connotation. The manna of this discourse represents the Jewish faith just as the *phrear* and the water pot represented the Samaritan religion in the former.

But this discourse does not end with Jesus straightening out the confusion between physical and spiritual bread. The multitude now fail to understand his reference to his Father, and say: "Is this not Jesus, the son of Joseph, whose father and mother we know?" Jesus then has to straighten them out, showing that he is from God, after which he again picks up the figure of the bread of life, adding the statement "and the bread which I shall give for the life of the world is my flesh." Once again the symbolism is misunderstood, and his listeners raise the question, "How can this man give us his flesh to eat?" This teaching causes not only the Jews to stumble, but even the disciples consider it a "hard saying," until he gives the key that it must be interpreted in spiritual terms--"It is the spirit that gives life; the flesh is of no avail; the words that I have spoken to you are spirit and life."

In the dialogue of John 8:31-59 the Jews are presented as the spiritually dull. The dialogue here turns on the fact that "father" can be used in a biological sense, or can be used for spiritual and ethical relationship-- doing what the father did. The dialogue has started earlier, and Jesus has claimed the authority of the Father for his teaching. Jesus then promised knowledge of the truth and freedom if they would "continue in my word." The Jews then claim to be descendants of Abraham, never in bondage to any one. Jesus tells them that if they were children of Abraham they would do what Abraham did. The Jews then shift their claim to having God as their Father, and Jesus counters by telling them that they have the devil as their father. They counter by accusing Jesus of having a demon, to which Jesus replies that he does not have a demon, but honors his Father, and that those who keep his word will never see death. They reject that, pointing out that Abraham had died and ask, incredulously, if Jesus is greater than Abraham, which leads to Jesus' assertion, "Before Abraham was, I am." The whole dialogue has turned on the ambiguity between a literal and symbolic meaning of the word "father," and Jesus uses the dialogue to stress his divine nature. Once again, he is the divine being moving through history.

Without attempting to look at all the passages in which the meaning of Jesus is missed, we may well look in closing at two more--the story of the raising of Lazarus, where there are several such misunderstandings, and the dialogue of chapter 14.

In the Lazarus incident (Jn. 11:1-44), the first misunderstanding takes place in a conversation between Jesus and his disciples. Jesus tells them that Lazarus has fallen asleep. He is using the term euphemistically, but the disciples misunderstand, and take it literally, suggesting that if Lazarus is asleep, it is a good thing. Thereupon Jesus explains that Lazarus is dead. The dullness of the disciples here is a literary device to make it possible for the Evangelist to make it clear, beyond all dispute, that Lazarus is dead, thus indicating the greatness of the sign which is to follow.

Jesus is next in conversation with Martha, and says to her, "Your brother will rise again" (Jn. 11:23). She fails to understand that he means at once, and speaks of a resurrection at the last day. This gives Jesus an opportunity to repudiate this teaching, in the oft quoted "I am the resurrection and the life; he who believes in me, though he die, yet shall he live, and whoever lives and believes in me shall never die" (Jn. 11:25-26). It is obvious that in the first reference to dying, physical death is involved--the believer may die physically but he lives spiritually. Just as obviously the second reference is to spiritual death--the believer may die physically but he never dies spiritually. Martha is asked if she believes this, but it is too much for her, and she simply affirms her belief in Jesus as the Christ. That Martha has failed to understand is brought out later in the story, when Jesus asks that the stone be moved away. She comments that the body will be decayed, for he has been dead for four days. Jesus retorts that he had promised that if she but believe, she should see the glory of God, and proceeds to complete his "sign."

In this discourse the dullness of Martha serves two functions. First of all, it gives Jesus an opportunity to teach that spiritual life begins not at death, but when one comes into a mystical relationship with him through belief. Secondly, it serves to keep the Johannine Martha in the same role as her synoptic counterpart. In Luke it is Martha who lacks spiritual insight and is troubled about many things, while Mary shows a sense of spiritual values in sitting and listening at the Master's feet (Lk. 10:38-42).

In the dialogue of chapter 14, Jesus opens with a promise to the disciples that he is going to prepare a place for them, so that " . . . where I am you may be also. And you know the way where I am going." Thomas fails to understand what Jesus is talking about, and protests that not knowing where Jesus is going, he cannot know the way. Thomas seems to be thinking of some physical journey, but his misunderstanding gives Jesus the opportunity to assert: "I am the way, and the truth, and the life; no one comes to the Father, but by me" (Jn. 14:6) and goes on to say "If you had known me, you would have known my Father also."

In a misunderstanding very similar to that of the Jews in chapter 8, Philip does not understand what Jesus means by "Father," and asks to be shown the Father. This gives Jesus an opportunity to teach unity with the Father. "He who has seen me has seen the Father."

The misunderstanding of both Thomas and Philip give Jesus an opportunity to teach about his divine nature, with the dialogue becoming a long monologue, as has been the case with so many of these dialogues with the spiritually dull.

While this study has not covered all the dialogues of the Fourth Gospel which are based on misunderstandings of a statement of Jesus, enough have been considered to give a feel of the Johannine style. The opponents of Jesus in these dialogues do not seem to be flesh and blood persons--they fit too nicely into a literary scheme which runs through the whole. Persons are slow at comprehending spiritual truths, but they are not as hopelessly dull as they appear in these Johannine dialogues. The style of these dialogues, with the conversationalists essentially "straw men," reminds one of the writings of the Greek philosophers or of the Greek-trained Justin who wrote *Dialogue with Trypho*. Since Jesus probably did not speak Greek, and since these dialogues depend upon ambiguities within Greek words, and since in nearly every instance one can find a saying or a situation which in some way reflects the Synoptics, it seem probable that they do not represent the actual words of Jesus, but the our editor's way of interpreting Jesus to the

Greek mind. Such persons were not necessarily Gentiles--they could be Jewish Christians of the diaspora who were trained in Greek ways of thought. Using a literary style that the Greek mind understood, these dialogues interpret Jesus as a divine being moving through history, expressing truths that could not be understood by his hearers, except as he painstakingly explained their deeper meaning.

Chapter III Endnotes

1.   Bernard (*op. cit.*, *ad loc.*) denies that the water of Jacob's well was "living water," but that is the basic meaning of *pēgē*--source of living water. Jesus later identifies himself as a *pēgē* of water springing up unto eternal life, and the whole point of the conversation hangs on the fact that the woman still thinks in terms of physical water.

2.   The italicized portion of the quotation departs from the RSV to indicate more fully the force of *chortazō*.

Chapter IV

Editorial Style and Structure

In this study it has been suggested that Matthew, Mark, and Luke are the reporters of the Good News about Jesus, and that John is the editor and interpreter of it. The reporters themselves were not eyewitnesses to the events they were describing, and so had to gather their information from various sources. Despite the fact that each writer used his sources in his own way, they did not work over the material sufficiently to make their works completely uniform in style and scholars can identify with considerable certainty material which came from Mark, from a source for the sayings of Jesus found in Matthew and Luke called "Q" by the scholars, and from sources unique to Matthew and Luke. The result of their method of writing may be described as a compilation rather than a composition.

When one turns to the Fourth Gospel, however, one finds that while its writer, too, used sources, he used them in such a way as to make his work into a literary unit.

This unity shows itself first of all in the way in which he used words. The Greek language was a highly developed language, which had different words to express fine shadings of meaning. It had, for instance, five words to express the idea of "seeing": *blepō, theaomai, theōreō, eidō,* and *horaō*. While these words might be used interchangeably, they had shades of meaning roughly equivalent to "seeing physically," "seeing with wonder," "seeing as a spectator," "to experience," and "to see with spiritual comprehension."[1] There are thirty-one sets of such apparent synonyms to be found in the Fourth

Gospel, and a careful study has revealed that in only one set, involving two words, are they used synonymously. Six sets, involving very common words, such as the words for "see," "speak," "come," and "know," are generally used with regard for their particular shades of meaning, but not always. This can be explained in part by the fact that words in common use tend to loose their exact connotation in any language, and failure to observe the difference does not necessarily indicate carelessness on the part of the author, but rather a natural linguistic development. It is significant, however, that seventy-one percent of the instances of failure to observe these shades of meaning occur in passages which have, for other reasons, been assigned by the Johannine scholar, Bacon, to the hand of a later reviser.

The remaining twenty-four sets of apparent synonyms are always used with a fine regard on the part of the author for their exact shade of meaning.[2] It becomes apparent that the first mark of the writer of this editorial on Jesus was a keen appreciation of the meaning of the words which he used. Failure on the part of translators generally to appreciate this fact has dulled the force and obscured the meaning of many passages in our ordinary English translations.

Another characteristic of the writer of John is a sense of movement. He always starts with something of lower meaning and moves through to a spiritual emphasis to be found at or near the close of a particular incident. This is well illustrated in any of the conversations with the spiritually dull studied in the last chapter, and also in the "signs." Another good illustration is found in the cleansing of the temple incident. Here the Evangelist has taken the incident reported in the Synoptics as belonging to the last week of Jesus' ministry, and has moved it to a place at the beginning of a Jerusalem ministry which follows immediately upon the opening of his public life in Galilee. In the Synoptics the cleansing of the temple starts the antagonism which leads to the death of Jesus, but in John it causes the Jews to ask for a "sign." Jesus replies with the statement, "Destroy this sanctuary, and I will raise it in three days!" (Jn. 2:19, Goodspeed).[3] This is generally accepted as the Johannine parallel of Mark 14:58, where it is charged at the trial of Jesus that he had said, "I will tear down this sanctuary built by men's hands, and in three days I will build another, made without hands."[4] There are, it is to be noted, important differences between the synoptic form and the form in John. The reference "built by men's hands" is left out, a very important omission for Johannine purposes, for the slow to comprehend consider it to be a reference to the physical temple, but in the Johannine form Jesus is speaking of his body. The situation has started out with the cleansing of a physical temple, in Greek, the *hieron*. Jesus has changed it to a conversation about the "sanctuary." This word is as good as any that we have in English to reflect the change in the Greek, where the word is *naos*, but it fails to carry the implications of the Greek. The Greek literally meant "the habitation of God," and was used by the Jews to refer to the inner courts of the temple, especially the Holy of Holies. The Jews take it in its literal meaning as applying to the temple, but, if verse 21 and 22 are from the Evangelist, it is intended to refer to the body of Jesus.[5] The Evangelist, by a deft change of words, has moved from the physical temple to a forecast of the resurrection. But this passage may have an even deeper significance. Commentators since the time of Theodore of Mopsuestia have suggested that the *hieron* stands for the old and spiritually dead religion of the Jews, while *naos* stands for the new spiritual religion of Jesus.[6] This suggestion has been strengthened by the discovery that the Qumran texts used the temple as a metaphor for the community.[7] If such an interpretation be accepted, verse 19 means

> Destroy this temple and worship, as ye have already begun to do by your desecration,--destroy it entirely, by putting the Messiah to death, and in three days I will build it new, *i.e.* not only rise from the dead, but also by the resurrection establish a new theocracy.[8]

The sense of movement which characterizes particular incidents in the Fourth Gospel is also found in the Gospel as a whole. One concept which furnishes this sense of movement is "my hour." As has been seen,[9] "my hour" is mentioned at the very beginning of Jesus' ministry and since it stands for the death, resurrection, and glorification of Jesus, the climax of the gospel, its early mention invites the reader to look forward with anticipation to the climax. The reader is reminded of "his hour" in 7:30 and 8:20, where Jesus cannot be arrested because "his hour had not yet come." This anticipated hour is finally reached in 12:23, where the statement is made "The hour has come for the Son of man to be glorified." The rest of the gospel is given over to the events which are a part of this glorification--death, resurrection, and return to the Father.

Another concept mentioned early in the gospel and near the end is that of being in someone's bosom. In 1:18 Jesus is "in the bosom of the Father," in 13:13 the Beloved Disciple is "lying close to the *bosom* of Jesus."[10] When one recalls the authority given to the Beloved Disciple at the cross, the point becomes clear. Authority in the church belongs to one who is close to Jesus as Jesus is in God.

Yet another concept that both provides movement and ties the gospel together as a unit is that of the descent of the Spirit. In 1:32 the Spirit is said to have descended and remained upon Jesus. In 20:22 Jesus says to his disciples, "Receive the Holy Spirit." With the end of Jesus' earthly ministry, the disciples now have spiritual authority.

Other concepts found at the beginning and end of the gospel include the idea of witness (Jn. 1:32-34; 19:35); believing giving life in his name (Jn. 1:12; 20:30); and the figure of Nicodemus (Jn. 3:1; 19:39).

This use of a common word or concept at the beginning and end of a work or portion thereof is technically called an *inclusio*. There are other *inclusios* in John, especially for some of the smaller units. This technique was not unknown in Greek literature, but it was much more common in Hebrew writing.

A definite sense of design is found in this book, not only in its movement, and in the literary pattern of the conversations with the spiritually dull that repeat themselves over and over again, always with the same general pattern, but also in a division of the book into an introduction and three parts.

Introduction--Ch. 1.

    A. Prologue

    B. Ministry of John and call of disciples.

Part I.   Early Ministry of Jesus--2:1-7:1.

Part II. Final Ministry of Jesus in Jerusalem--7:2-12:50.

    "My time has not yet come."

Part III. Glorification--13:1-20:30.

    "Jesus, knowing that his hour was come"

  Appendix--Ch. 21

The remarkable relationships between the introductory paragraphs of the three parts, 2:4ff., 7:6ff., and 13:1ff., have generally been overlooked. All three open with a reference to "my hour" or "my time." All involve a display of his Messiahship. All come at critical points in his life--at the beginning of his ministry, the beginning of his Judean ministry, and the beginning of his passion. In all three there is a close relation to the order of events given in the Synoptics: the *ti emoi kai soi* of 2:4 seems likely to be inspired by the *ti hēmin kai soi* of Mark 1:24;[11] the story of Jesus separating himself from his brothers before going to Jerusalem may very likely be inspired by the statement about no man leaving home and brothers found in all three Synoptics (Mark 10:30 and parallels) *immediately* before Jesus sets out for Jerusalem; while the footwashing incident, with its humbling of Peter, seems to be but a dramatic form of the Lukan ". . .let the greatest among you become as the youngest, and leader as one who serves. . . . I am among you as one who serves" (Lk. 22:26f.). John follows Luke 22:31f. in making Peter the object of this lesson in humility.

There are additional similarities between the introductory paragraphs of Part I and Part II that do not carry over to Part III. In both, Jesus is requested to do something by a member of his family. In both, he apparently refuses with a reference to "my hour" or "my time," and then proceeds to do the thing which he apparently has just refused, with the suggestion that he and the members of his family have nothing in common with each other.

Such similarities as these can hardly be regarded as accidental. The man who was writing these passages had a definite scheme and plan which he was following. He was a skilled literary craftsman who had a literary pattern which guided him as he wrote. This, incidentally, rather thoroughly discredits the partition theories of Wendt, Wellhausen,[12] and Broome.[13]

The close relationship of these three sections of the gospel to each other and to their synoptic sources reveals the way in which the Evangelist treated his sources, for it shows him adapting synoptic material to fit into the literary pattern of his work. When he is through with the synoptic material, his story and that of the synoptic writers could pass for different incidents-- indeed, they universally do so pass--but in all three cases there is a common theme with the synoptic material, a common location in the life of

Jesus, and in one instance a common saying, though from different lips, and in the others enough similarity to show that the Evangelist is not compiling from sources not known elsewhere, but that he is interpreting from the synoptic record.

The unity, the sense of movement both within particular passages and through the gospel as a whole, the definite sense of literary pattern and design, and the way in which synoptic material is freely treated to bring it into the literary pattern, all show this work to be a composition rather than a compilation. This evidence, especially the evidence of the freedom with which synoptic sources have been treated, suggests agreement with the views of Clement and Origen that the Fourth Evangelist may often have preserved "spiritual truth. . . , as one might say, in the material falsehood."[14] The evidence of conscious literary style is so great as to lead to the conviction that the writer had no qualms about following the accepted literary practice of his day in creating situations and sayings which he felt interpreted his subject. He starts with historical material largely from the synoptic tradition, even as the portrait artist starts with the features of a real face, but the result is in both cases an interpretation rather than a reproduction. Such a method of writing is technically known as midrashic. Midrash was a Jewish method of interpreting and expanding on sacred texts to bring out their meaning for a new age. This method allowed for considerable development and expansion of the original material. The evidence would suggest that the author of the Fourth Gospel is familiar with this method and uses it.[15]

Chapter IV Endnotes

1.   *Supra*, 23f.

2.   Maynard, *Function of Apparent Synonyms and Ambiguous Words*, 337-344.

3.   Goodspeed, Edgar J., *The New Testament, An American Translation.* (Chicago: University of Chicago Press, 1935), *ad loc*. Goodspeed here reflects the Greek more accurately than does the RSV.

4.   *Ibid., ad loc.* The critical word is *naos*, which is better translated "sanctuary," rather than "temple."

5.   Note that *naos* is used with the same double meaning in the Markan statement which the Evangelist is here developing.

6.   Schaff lists Kuinoel, Tholuck, Meyer, Olshausen, Stier, and Brückner as supporting this view. Lange, *op. cit.. ad loc.* See also Macgregor, *op. cit., ad loc.*

7.   Schnackenburg, Rudolf, *The Gospel According to St John*, K. Smith, trans. (New York: Seabury Press, 1979) I, *ad loc*.

8.   Lange, *op. cit.*, ad. loc.

9.   *Supra*, 14.

10.   The RSV reads "breast" rather than "bosom," but the word in Greek is the same in each verse.

11.   *Supra*, 14ff.

12.   The views of Wendt and Wellhausen are presented and criticized by Macgregor, *op. cit.*, xl.

13.   Broome, Edwin C., Jr., "The Sources of the Fourth Gospel," *Journal of Biblical Literature*, (June 1944): 107-21.

14.   Origin, *Commentary on John*, i.9; x.1-4.

15.   Material in this chapter draws heavily upon some of the conclusions of my dissertation, especially pp. 428-430, but new matter has been added. On Midrash, see my forthcoming book, *John, a Midrash on the Synoptics.*

Chapter V

The Author's use of Symbols

Yet another literary characteristic of the Fourth Gospel is the use of symbols. Some of the symbolism of the gospel is discussed elsewhere--the new wine of the miracle of Cana as a symbol for the new religion of Christianity with the water pots as symbols of Judaism;[1] the five husbands of the woman of Samaria as a symbol of the Samaritan Torah, her water pots a symbol of her religion, and the living water promised by Jesus a symbol of the new, true faith;[2] in the scene at the cross, the mother of Jesus as a symbol for the church and the beloved disciple a symbol for authentic church leaders[3]-- but there are additional important symbols that need to be discussed.

The first is the dual symbolism of "light" and "darkness." This is first clearly stated in the prologue:

> In him was life, and the life was the light of men. The light shines in the darkness, and the darkness has not overcome it. There was a man sent from God, whose name was John. He came for testimony, to bear witness to the light, that all might believe through him. He was not the light, but came to bear witness to the light. The true light that enlightens every man was coming into the world (Jn. 1:4-9).

In six short verses "light" appears six times, and "enlighten" once. Obviously this is a concept that the author wants to stress! Christ, the Logos, has already been identified with creation, and creation, light, and life are closely identified in Old Testament thought. The logos is said to be the "true light." "True," in Johannine thought, means the ultimately real. The idea is that with the logos God has come into the world. Further, darkness--life without God--has not been able to put out the light. The purpose of this light coming into the world is to bring salvation--"But to all who received him, who believed in his name, he gave power to become children of God" (Jn. 1:12).

Having been stressed in the Prologue, this idea of Jesus as the light of the world runs throughout the gospel. The Nicodemus story comes to its conclusion with:

> And this is the judgment, that the light has come into the world, and men loved darkness rather than light, because their deeds were evil. For every one who does evil hates the light, lest his deeds should be exposed. But he who does what is true comes to the light, that it may be clearly seen that his deeds have been wrought in God (Jn. 3:19-21).

This could be interpreted simply as meaning that evil men do not like to have their deeds exposed to public view. This is practically a truism, but John means much more than that. Both the idea of judgment and the idea of the "light come into the world" suggest that the "light" is Christ. Dodd was certainly correct when he suggested that "he who does what is true" indicates "one who belongs to the realm of reality."[4] One who lives in the realm of reality lives in the light and his actions are done in harmony with God.

The passage is also significant because it suggests that the dualism between light and darkness is essentially ethical rather than ontological. One lives in the light or in the darkness on the basis of what one does.

The Nicodemus dialogue opened with the statement that "this man came to Jesus by night. . ."(Jn. 3:2). In any other gospel this would be correctly regarded as a simple reference to the time of day in which the event is taking place, but in John's gospel it must be regarded as having symbolic significance. One who comes by night belongs to the darkness. Nicodemus, though he was a ruler of the Jews, was spiritually "in the dark" because he was without Christ.

"Light" next appears in 5:35. Here Jesus is talking about the fact that he bears witness to himself, but also that John the Baptist bore witness to him. "You sent to John and he has born witness to the truth. . . . He was a burning and shining lamp, and you were willing to rejoice for a while in his light. But the testimony that I have is greater than that of John; . . ."

This passage is part of the polemic of this gospel against the followers of John the Baptist. The book of Acts indicates that there were those who knew the baptism of John but not that of Jesus. In other words, there was a sect made up of followers of John the Baptist. The author of the Fourth Gospel wants that group to know that John's only purpose was to witness to Jesus. His "light" was a temporary light; one recalls the Prologue, "He (John) was not the light, but came to bear witness to the light" (Jn. 1:8).

The famous "I am the light of the world" passage occurs at 8:12, where Jesus goes on to say "...he who follows me will not walk in darkness, but will have the light of life." Again, as in the prologue, "light" and "life" are closely associated with each other. The idea here is clearly salvational. Jesus as the light of the world makes it possible for one not to walk in darkness--not to live apart from God--but to have life. There are three words for "life" in Greek: *bios*, which is not used in John; *psuchē*, which could be translated "physical life," and *zoē*, which in John always carries the connotation of "spiritual life." It is this last term which is used in this passage.

The next passage where "light" is found deals with the idea that the light is tied to the life of Jesus. Jn. 9:5 states it succinctly: "As long as I am in the world, I am the light of the world." The same idea is also found at 12:35-36:

> The light is with you for a little longer. Walk while you have the light, lest the darkness overtake you; he who walks in the darkness does not know where he goes. While you have the light, believe in the light, that you may become sons of light.

50

This passage also contains the emphasis on salvation. One should make use of the time, in order to become "sons of light," which is simply another way of saying, as it was said in the prologue, "sons of God."

In the Lazarus story, Jesus, before he goes to Bethany, has a conversation with the disciples in which he notes that there are "twelve hours in the day," and that one who "walks in the day. . . does not stumble, because he sees the light of this world."

This could be interpreted as a simple time reference. If one walks in the light of the sun, it is a lot safer than to walk after sunset. But such an interpretation is rather meaningless in the context.[5] The disciples have just warned Jesus that the Jews are seeking his life. The "light of this world" is not the sun but the Son. As Barrett well says: "In addition to the surface meaning John intends to suggest that in the light given by Jesus men walk safely; apart from him is darkness, in which men plunge into sin (9:39-41)."[6]

The final reference to "light," 12:46, is, when read with the entire paragraph for which it is the topic sentence (12:46-50), a fitting summary of the significance of "light" for this gospel. First, Jesus says that "I have come as light into the world, that whoever believes in me may not remain in darkness"--the purpose of his coming was to bring salvation. But, if one does not hear and do his words, one is judged. Jesus has spoken what the Father commanded, and "his commandment is eternal life." Once again, the stress is ethical. One walks in the light by doing what Jesus has commanded, the doing of Jesus' words brings eternal life because he has been faithful to God. Failure to do what Jesus has taught brings final judgment.

In addition to the reference to "night" in the Nicodemus story, already noted, such reference is found in two other places. The first is in the story of the calming of the storm (6:16-21), which has already been discussed.[7]

The same kind of double emphasis on time is found in the story of Mary Magdalene at the tomb (20:1-18): "Early, . . .it was still dark." Again, this could possibly be only a time reference--but why the double stress? Mary is still without Jesus. She thinks "They have taken the Lord out of the tomb" (20:2). She is "in the dark" until, later in the story, she can say "I have seen the Lord" (20:18).

While 13:30 lacks the double emphasis found above, it may be much more than a time reference when one reads of Judas: "So, after receiving the morsel, he immediately went out; and it was night." The next reference to Judas is at 18:3, where "Judas. . . went there with lanterns and torches and weapons." While this may be only a time reference, Judas' deed is certainly in the realm of evil, and the reference to night, reenforced by the stress on lanterns and torches, may well have symbolic as well as literal significance.[8]

There is considerable debate among the scholars as to the source of this light-darkness dualism. Does it come from John's Jewish heritage, or is it of Greek origin? In the Old Testament, light is the first thing to be created and it is often associated with manifestations of God. One thinks, for instance, of the burning bush, or of the glow of Moses' face after his encounter with God. The word of God can be referred to as a "lamp to my feet and a light to my path" (Ps. 119:105). The writings of the rabbis continued this, using "light" both of the law, and as a name for the Messiah.[9] The Dead Sea Scrolls use this dualism--so much so that when they were first found, some scholars argued that John was directly dependent on them.

But on the other hand, there is much in Hellenistic literature and in pagan religions, especially from Persia, that reflect this dualism. In the Hermetic literature one finds that the Word is the active agent of creation, that the Word is the Son of God and the light of men. Philo, an Alexandrian Jew who sought to interpret Judaism in terms understandable to the Greek mind, speaks of God as light. As Barrett comments, "The parallelism between John, Philo, and the *Hermetica* is very remarkable."[10]

So, is John dependent on Hellenistic thought, or on Jewish thought in his use of this dualism? The answer is probably both, but neither in any conscious way. The dualism was prevalent in the culture of the time. The metaphor of light is used in several places in the Synoptic Gospels (Mk. 4:21f.; Mt.4:16; 5:14). Barrett is undoubtedly correct when he suggests that in his use of the phrase "light of the world," John "stands within the primitive Christian tradition."[11]

Another word that carries tremendous symbolic meaning for John is "hour." Some attention has already been given to this in connection with the discussion of the miracle of Cana. The "hour" for this gospel is the time of

Jesus' crucifixion, resurrection, and ascension, which are thought of as a single event--Jesus' glorification or return to the Father.

There are times in the Fourth Gospel when "hour" is used to indicate time of day, as in 4:6, where it is said that it was "about the sixth hour." It can also be used to indicate time as in the statement to the Samaritan woman: ". . . the hour is coming when neither on this mountain nor in Jerusalem will you worship the Father. . . . . But the hour is coming, and now is, when the true worshipers will worship the Father in spirit and truth, . . . "(Jn. 4:21-23). But this statement is much more than an indication of time. Lindars has suggested that "the hour is coming" is a technical expression in John for the eschatological event, and that by the adding of "and now is" in verse 23, that event is brought into the present by the person of Jesus.[12] This tie to the eschatological event is verified by looking at 5:25, where it is said: ". . . the hour is coming and now is, when the dead will hear the voice of the Son of God, and those who hear will live," and at 12:23, where the event is no longer future, but present: "The hour has come for the Son of Man to be glorified." What follows makes it clear that this is a reference to the crucifixion, resurrection, and return to the Father--for John a single event. So the "time" indicated to the Samaritan woman by "hour" is a very specific time--the time of the new age brought about by Jesus' glorification.

There are two significant passages before "The hour has come" of 12:23 that need attention. At 7:6 Jesus tells his brothers, who have been urging him to go up to Jerusalem:

> My time has not yet come, but your time is always here. The world cannot hate you, but it hates me because I testify of it that its works are evil. Go to the feast yourselves; I am not going up to this feast, for my time has not yet fully come.

Surprisingly, after being told in verse 9 that Jesus remained in Galilee, we are told in verse 10 that he did go up to the feast, "not publicly, but in private."

Does "time" here equal "hour?" Jesus does not want to go up to the feast publicly because it is not yet time for his death? Most commentators believe that "time" is here synonymous with "hour." If this is indeed so, it is, contrary to the view of most commentators, unusual--for John has a fine sense for precise shades of meaning.[13] The close association of this passage with the Cana story has been noted above, which would seem to argue for "time" to equal "hour." But, whereas Jesus' "hour" represents the time of the passion, it is possible that "time" here means that it is not yet time for Jesus to manifest himself--which is what his brothers have been urging him to do.[14] "Time" and "hour" are not synonyms after all!

The other passage that should be considered before looking at the passages dealing with when the hour has come, is the reference to "twelve hours in the day" (Jn. 11:9) in the Lazarus story. Just as the "light of this world" turned out to be more than the physical sun, this is more than a casual observation of the length of a day. Jesus' hour has not yet come, and therefore he can go to Judea even if the Jews are seeking to stone him. His "twelve hours" have not run out!

All of the references to "hour" at 12:23, 27; 13:1; 16:32 and 17:1 are references to Jesus' glorification. Of particular interest is the reference at 12:27: "Now is my soul troubled. And what shall I say? 'Father save me from this hour'? No, for this purpose I have come to this hour." This passage has some close similarities with Mark 14:35b-36. Jesus has been said to be greatly distressed and troubled (not the same Greek word as that translated "troubled" in John) and says "My soul is very sorrowful. . ." (Mk. 14:34). He then prays "that, if it were possible *the hour* might pass from him. . . yet (*all'*) not what I will but what thou wilt."

It has been suggested, probably correctly, that John gets his whole concept of the hour as the time of Jesus' passion and glorification from this passage, which with this wording, is unique to Mark. There seems to be a striking difference between Mark and John in that in Mark Jesus would like to be delivered from his fate but is willing to accept God's will. The strong "No" of the English translation of John makes it seem that the Johannine Jesus cannot even entertain such a prayer for deliverance. But, as Lindars points out, the Greek behind the "No", is *alla*, literally "but" or "yet," the same word as in Mark 14:36.[15] John has no Gethsemane--his Jesus is too divine for that--both the concept of "the hour" as the time of glorification and the petition of 12:27 may be a midrashic development on Mark.

There are probably other symbolic references in the Fourth Gospel. Culpepper has argued that the "core symbols" of the Gospel are "light and darkness, ordinary water and living water, plain bread and true bread,"[16] but "water" is used in a number of different ways, as has been seen. It is probably most frequently a symbol for baptism, and in that role will be treated in a discussion of the sacraments. When contrasted with "living water" it is a tool for setting up a dialogue, as is the contrast between "plain bread" and "true bread," the latter also having sacramental significance. It is, however, not important to determine which are the most significant symbols in this gospel. Rather, it is necessary to realize how important it is to look for the symbolism if one is to understand the significance of this material. If one takes these terms in their literal rather than in their symbolic sense, much of the significance of the message is lost.

Chapter V Endnotes

1.   *Supra.*, 18.

2.   *Supra.*, 31.

3.   *Infra*, 60

4.   Dodd, C. H., *The Interpretation of the Fourth Gospel* (Cambridge: University Press, 1953), 210.

5.   Schnackenberg (*op. cit.* II, 325) prefers this literal interpretation.

6.   Barrett, C. K., *The Gospel According to St. John*, 2nd. ed. (Philadelphia: The Westminster Press, 1978), *ad loc.*

7.   *Supra*, 22.

8.   Culpepper, R. Alan, *Anatomy of the Fourth Gospel: A Study in Literary Design* (Philadelphia: Fortress Press, 1983) 192, follows this same interpretation. I became aware of Culpepper's treatment after my draft was written. Culpepper also notes that in ch. 21 the disciples have no luck in fishing while it is still dark. The carrying through of this symbol does not change my view of ch. 21 as an appendix written by a different person who was almost certainly also a member of the Johannine school, but writing at a later time.

9.   I am following Barrett here. His excellent discussion is found in connection with his treatment of 8:12. His reference for the rabbinic material is to Strack and Billerbeck, *Kommentar zum Neuen Testament aus Talmud und Midrasch*, I, 67, 151, 161, II, 428.

10.   *Ibid.*, 336.

11.   *Ibid.*, 337.

12.   Lindars, Barnabas, *The Gospel of John* The New Century Bible Commentary (Grand Rapids: Eerdmans, 1971) *ad loc. Cf.* Barrett, *op. cit., ad loc.* These two scholars complement each other on this passage.

13.   Maynard, *Apparent Synonyms and Ambiguous Words.*

14.   *Ibid.*, 199-203.

15.   Lindars, *op. cit., ad loc.*

16.   Culpepper, *op. cit.*, 200.

Chapter VI

Peter and the Beloved Disciple[1]

In the Synoptic Gospels Peter is clearly the leader of the disciples, but when one turns to the Fourth Gospel, there is an obvious depreciation of his importance. In the Synoptics Peter and his brother Andrew are the first disciples chosen by Jesus, but in John, Andrew and an unnamed disciple of John the Baptist are the first to follow Jesus and "abide with him." While the account clearly says that they "abode the rest of the day" with Jesus, "abiding" in John's Gospel is a spiritual relationship, into which they have entered. The next day Andrew goes and calls his brother Simon, and he is promptly named by Jesus "Cephas" or "Peter," an incident which according to Matthew did not happen until the disciples are in Caesarea Philippi, just before Jesus starts on the final journey to Jerusalem.

Peter is next mentioned in 6:8, but only as the brother of Andrew. Whereas the other gospels do not identify the disciple with whom Jesus converses about the food for the multitude, John clearly identifies him as Andrew, the brother of Peter. The use of Peter to identify Andrew suggests that the author is aware that Peter is well known, but this knowledge does not rest on any publicity that he himself has provided.

Peter next appears in 6:68, in the Johannine equivalent of the Caesarea Philippi incident. Jesus is at Capernaum and notes that many are turning away from him, and asks the disciples if they, too, will go away. Peter answers, "Lord, to whom shall we go? You have the words of eternal life; and we have believed, and have come to know, that you are the Holy One of

God." This confession is considerably expanded from the brief "You are the Christ" recorded in Mark, but the expansion, in terms of "words of eternal life," is characteristic of John, who has followed the Synoptics in making Peter the spokesman for the disciples. It is significant to note that this is the only time in the Fourth Gospel that Peter is the spokesman for the twelve,[2] and that here John has omitted any praise of Peter on the part of Jesus. The name Peter has already been given, and there is no hint of anything like the statement, "on this rock I will build my church."

Peter next appears in chapter 13, in the account of the foot-washing. This is a highly symbolic passage in which John plays upon the two Greek words for "wash," *niptō*, which meant to wash a part of one's body, and *louō*, which meant to bathe the entire body. Peter protests the washing of his feet by Jesus, then asks that his hands and his face be washed, also, and Jesus replies that he who has bathed only needs but to have his feet washed. "Bathing" in this passage is undoubtedly a symbol for baptism, and the foot-washing a symbol for the Eucharist in that it is "the giving of the Lord himself in service to humanity."[3] The sacrament, he is saying, is empty unless it is accompanied by the Spirit which renders life "clean." The Evangelist is insisting on the importance of the sacraments, but even more he is insisting on the necessity of a spiritual experience behind them. In this incident Peter is spiritually dull, and the story does nothing to enhance his position.

Later on in the same chapter, while the disciples are still in the upper room, Peter is further depreciated, first by his position at the table,[4] and second by having him fail to understand the statement of Jesus that he is going where they cannot follow. This conversation follows the Johannine pattern of conversations with the spiritually dull, and Jesus utilizes the opportunity to predict the denial.

Peter next enters the story in the Garden when he still fails to understand that Jesus must "drink the cup which the Father has given," so he cuts off the ear of the servant of the high priest. In reporting this rather uncomplimentary incident it is John alone who identifies Peter as the one who wields the sword – the other gospels simply report that it was done by "one of those who stood by."

After the arrest of Jesus, Peter and an unidentified disciple follow Jesus to the house of the high priest. Peter gains admittance to the courtyard only because the other "disciple was known to the high priest" (Jn. 18:15), and then having gained admittance, disgraces himself by denying his Lord three times. There are a number of differences between John and the parallel stories in the Synoptics, two of which are important to this discussion. In the Synoptics Peter denies *knowing* Jesus, while in John he denies his *discipleship*, which, from the Johannine perspective is far more serious. Secondly, in the Synoptics Peter "broke down and wept" (Mk. 14:72; *cf.* Lk. 22:62; Mt. 26:75) when he realized what he had done, while the Johannine Peter shows no remorse or repentance for his act.

The final appearance of Peter in the genuine Johannine material is at 20:2, where Peter and the beloved disciple run together to the tomb. This passage will be examined in greater detail after a study of the appearances of the "beloved disciple." It is sufficient to note here that while Peter is the first to the tomb, he only sees, while the "beloved disciple" sees *and believes*. Further, there is no record of an appearance of the Risen Christ to Peter as in Paul's account of the resurrection.

The "beloved disciple" first appears, at least with this designation, in the account of the events following the foot-washing. Jesus has just predicted that one will betray him, and, one reads:

> The disciples looked at one another, uncertain of whom he spoke. One of his disciples, whom Jesus loved, was lying close to the *bosom*[5] of Jesus; so Simon Peter beckoned to him and said, "Tell us who it is of whom he speaks." So lying thus, close to the breast of Jesus, he said to him, "Lord, who is it?" (Jn. 13:22-25).

Traditionally the beloved disciple has been identified as John, son of Zebedee, but this identification is based on the statement of John 21:24, "This is the disciple who is bearing witness to these things, and who has written these things," combined with the tradition that John, son of Zebedee, was the one who wrote this Gospel, or is at least the beloved disciple, responsible for the tradition passed on to one of his followers, who actually wrote the gospel. This view is returning to scholarly favor in some quarters,[6] but against this must be noted not only the arguments against Johannine authorship already considered, but the fact that chapter 21 is almost universally regarded as a late appendix, and that even if it is accepted, its identification of the beloved disciple as John is not explicit but only by rather indirect implication.

Those who recognize the improbability of the validity of the traditional identification have made a large number of suggestions as to whom this man may have been. The suggestion made by Sandy that he was a young Jerusalemite is one that has found wide acceptance; others have suggested that he was the rich young ruler, or Lazarus, or Nicodemus,[7] or the host at whose home the Last Supper was eaten.[8] None of these identifications can, as Garvie well notes,[9] be proven, and many scholars have suggested that the beloved disciple must be regarded primarily not as a historical person, but as some kind of symbol. Bacon, whose position was similar to that held by Jülicher,[10] maintained that he was "that ideal disciple whom Jesus would choose and who reads his soul aright."[11] Titus has suggested that the beloved disciple is a shadowy figure, purposely unidentified to serve the needs of this gospel, and has asked if he is in a sense a "second Jesus" who is not a divine figure on the cross – a sort of a Docetic view.[12] Scott has made the suggestion that the beloved disciple is the prototype of the future church.[13] The research of the present writer leads to the conclusion that he is a symbol for the leadership of the Johannine church – he is any leader who is in the bosom of Jesus as Jesus is in the bosom of God; he is any leader who is possessed by the Paraclete, the Comforter, the Holy Spirit. The mother of Jesus symbolizes the Church over which he has authority. This is close to Titus' suggestion that he is "a second Jesus," but not in any docetic sense.

The word development in the passage describing the beloved disciple's first appearance is especially significant for this interpretation. He is introduced with the comment that he is "on the bosom" of Jesus. While it is technically possible that this expression only means that he was reclining against the full folds of Jesus' robe,[14] the Johannine pattern of mentioning early in the gospel things which will be used later invites us to remember that in 1:18 it was said of Jesus that he was "in the bosom of the Father." While the two expressions are not in the same grammatical form, the one of 1:18

being *eis* with the accusative and the one in 13:23 being *en* with the dative, this does not mean that the two are not to be considered in relation to each other. It seems possible that the Evangelist is here saying that just as Jesus was in the bosom of the Father from the beginning, the beloved disciple, i.e., the spirit-possessed church leadership, is in the bosom of Christ, the difference in grammar perhaps was meant to indicate that the relationship between the beloved disciple and Jesus is not as complete or as eternal as that between Jesus and God.[15]

It is to be further noted that two verses after the first mention of the beloved disciple as "on the bosom of Jesus" it is said that "he leaned back from where he lay, on Jesus' breast" (Jn. 13:15, Goodspeed). Here the Greek shifts from *kolpos*, bosom, to *stēthos*, breast, and this may be regarded as a deliberate shift to a word suggesting only physical proximity to indicate that the higher or symbolic meaning has been completed, and the writer is going on to other things.

If this symbolical interpretation is accepted, it is important to note the depreciation of Peter involved in this passage. It is the beloved disciple, not Peter, who is next to Jesus, and when Peter wants to know the answer to a question, he must get his information through the mediation of the beloved disciple.

It has already been noted that after the arrest of Jesus, Peter gained admittance to the courtyard of the high priest only through the mediation of an "other disciple." It is a matter of considerable debate as to whether or not this "other disciple" is to be considered as identical with the beloved disciple. He well fits the role of the beloved disciple as established in the first incident in that Peter gets something through him, and in that Peter is therefore subordinate to him, but since the author has not made the identification explicit, he may only be saying that Peter is subordinate to other disciples besides the "beloved" one.

In 19:26 the beloved disciple is standing near the cross, and the words to the mother of Jesus—who is never called Mary in this gospel—"Woman, behold your son!" and to the disciple, "Behold, your mother!," are spoken. It has already been suggested that this incident is related to the disavowal by

Jesus of his filial relationship at the beginning of his ministry (Jn. 2:4), with the beloved disciple taking the place of Jesus.[16]

It is difficult to be certain about the symbolism here. It can be argued that the beloved disciple stands for the church, in which case this can be seen as legitimatizing the beginning of Maryology. While the writer of this gospel knew from synoptic sources that there were strained relationships between Jesus and his family at the outset of his ministry, he also knew that Mary, the mother of Jesus, was active in the early church.[17] He may be saying that Mary was not only in the church, but that she had a very special place in the church, and that here is an indication of the beginning of Maryology. He may be saying that the *whole church* is responsible for the care of his mother, i.e., for carrying out Jesus' obligations.

There are, however, real problems with this interpretation. The fact that the Evangelist never calls the mother of Jesus "Mary" would seem to argue against it. Further, it has been argued above that the beloved disciple is not a symbol for the whole church, but for the leadership of the church. In the book of Revelation one finds the mother of Jesus used as a symbol for the messianic community, including the church (Rev. 12:13-17), and while there are vast differences between the Johannine gospel and the Revelation, they are both attributed to a "John," and *may* come from the same community. The church is the body of Christ on earth. According to this interpretation, the bodily Jesus disavows the importance of the incarnation for the period of his ministry, but makes the church the new incarnation on his return to glory. This church is under the control of the beloved disciple – anyone close to Jesus as Jesus is to God, and not Peter or James, the brother of Jesus, or anyone else.

The beloved disciple next appears at 20:2.[18] Here he is again in the company of Peter, and again, the author's use of words is highly significant. Peter and the other disciple run to the tomb, and the beloved disciple gets there first. But with some reverence for holy things he *glances*[19] in and sees (*blepō*) the linen clothes. Peter, however, rushes into the tomb, and observes (*theōreō*) the cloths and the napkin, whereon the other disciple enters, sees with spiritual comprehension (*horaō*), and believes. With deference to tradition, Peter is allowed to be the first to enter the tomb. But the choice of verbs makes it clear that Peter is being depreciated and that the beloved disciple is credited with having more spiritual comprehension, and as being the first to embrace the resurrection faith.

In view of the prominent role played by Peter in the Synoptics and in the early chapters of Acts, one is forced to ask, why this depreciation of Peter and exaltation of the beloved disciple which is carried so consistently through the book? If the symbolism of the beloved disciple as the charismatic church leadership is accepted, one does not have far to look for the answer, for Peter was very early associated with Rome, and the Roman church very early based its authority on Peter. Could it not be that through this gospel the leader of the Johannine community of churches is saying (1) that Peter (i.e., Rome) needed a lesson in humility, (2) that Peter (i.e., Rome) was not superior to, but subservient to, the total church, (3) that Mary (i.e., the whole church) was responsible for carrying on his work, and that (4) no one section of the church could claim priority for the faith? There is no sure way of knowing where this Johannine community of churches was located, but perhaps it was located in Alexandria, a church that was always cool toward the claims of Rome.[20]

The probability of such an interpretation is supported when one looks at chapter 21, which comes after the statement of 20:30, which is so obviously the original end of the gospel. When one looks at that chapter, Peter is the leader of the disciples: he hauls the net--symbol of the world mission of the church--to shore, and he is reinstated in his role as shepherd of Christ's flock. The beloved disciple is bowed out of the picture so far as any present commission is concerned ("What is that to you?"), but is identified as the author of the book. Does it not appear that someone is trying to make the Gospel of John palatable to the Church at Rome, which historically was the last to accept it, by (1) reasserting the importance of Peter, and (2) by suggesting that the book had apostolic authorship?

64

Chapter VI Endnotes

1.   For a more technical study on this theme, see Maynard, "The Role of Peter in the Fourth Gospel," *New Testament Studies*, 30 (1984), 531-548.

2.   Bernard, *op. cit., ad loc.*

3.   Macgregor, *op. cit., ad loc.*

4.   For development of this, see below, p. 61.

5.   "Bosom" is here substituted for the RSV "breast" to indicate that a different word is found in the Greek here than the one translated "breast" in the next sentence. The word translated "bosom" is *kolpos*, which is also used in John 1:18 to indicate the relationship of Jesus and God.

6.   Among scholars who hold this view are Brown *John*, I-XII, (xcii-cii), and Schnackenburg (*op. cit.*, I, 75-104). Lindars (*op. cit.*, 28-34) rejects this view. In this age of ecumenical scholarship one is reluctant even to make the suggestion, but both Brown and Schnackenburg are Roman Catholic scholars, and Schnackenburg makes much of the importance of John, son of Zebedee, authorship to "the magisterium." Is a confessional stance influencing their view?

7.   These suggestions are reviewed by Alfred Garvie, "John," *Abingdon Bible Commentary* (N. Y.: Abingdon Press, 1929), 1065.

8.   Robinson, Benjamin W., *The Gospel of John.* (N. Y.: Macmillan, 1925), 27.

9.   Garvie, *loc. cit.*

10.   Jülicher, Adolf, *An Introduction to the New Testament*, Janet Ward, trans. (London: Smith, Elder, and Co., 1904), 413.

11.   Bacon, Benjamin W., *Introduction to the New Testament*(N. Y.: The Macmillan Co., 1924), 326, 320.

12.   Titus, Eric, Professor, Religion 227b, University of Southern California, Fall semester, 1947-48. Titus has since suggested privately that the beloved disciple may be the Matthias of Acts 1:26.

13.   Scott, *op. cit.*, 144.

14.   Westcott, *op. cit., ad loc.* Cf. Alfred Plummer, *The Gospel According to St. John. The Cambridge Bible for Schools and College*, J. J. S. Perowne, ed. (Cambridge: University Press, 1906), *ad loc.*; and Lange, *op. cit., ad loc.*

15.   Maynard, *Apparent Synonyms and Ambiguous Words*, 177-180.

16.   *Supra*, 15.

17.   The activity of Mary is mentioned in the book of Acts, but the Evangelist is not necessarily dependent upon this source for his knowledge of the importance of Mary.

18.   The word *phileö* is used in describing the beloved disciple only in this verse, but on the basis of the research done by Benjamin B. Warfield "The

Terminology of Love in the New Testament," *The Princeton Theological Review*, 16:1-44 [January and April, 1918 153-203], reexamined with particular reference to Johannine material by Maynard (*Apparent Synonyms and Ambiguous Words*, 266-71), no great significance can be placed on this shift. Warfield clearly shows that by New Testament times *agapaō* was the general word for love, while *phileō* indicated an emphasis on the fact that the relationship brought pleasure to those involved.

19.   The usual translation is "stooping to look in," but *parakupteō* is consistently used in the LXX of "peeping," and the idea would seem to be that he gave a quick glance. Maynard, *Apparent Synonyms and Ambiguous Words*, 145.

20.   See Brown, *The Community of the Beloved Disciple*. Brown does not identify the churches of the opposition as Rome, but calls them the Apostolic Churches. Brown stresses that the Johannine Community differed with the Apostolic Churches not only over authority, but also over christology, eschatology, and pneumatology.

Chapter VII

"Abide in me, and I in You"[1]

The idea of "abiding" is a key thought in Johannine literature. Brown has shown that the Greek word, *menein*, appears in the Gospel of John forty times as opposed to twelve times in the Synoptics.[2] It appears in the Johannine Epistles an additional twenty-seven times, so it was clearly a favorite with the Johannine community.

The word is variously translated in our English versions. Minear, following Caird, notes that *The New English Bible* uses nine different English words to translate it.[3] This is unfortunate, because much of the continuity that the Evangelist intended is lost by the failure to be consistent in the translation. The basic meaning of the word is "abide," but in Johannine usage it connotes a permanent, mutual indwelling.[4]

The word first appears in the gospel in the witness of John the Baptist and the conversation between Jesus and two of John's disciples which follows (1:32-41). This is another illustration of the way in which the Evangelist very early introduces an idea that will be developed more fully later on in the gospel. John's witness is "I saw the Spirit . . . descend from heaven and it abode (KJ, RSV reads "remained") upon him" (1:32). The spirit has been described as "like a dove," and on the surface it might appear that John sees the dove of the spirit perching on Jesus' shoulder for a long time, but the next line makes it clear that something more is involved. John testifies that God has told him that "He on whom you see the Spirit descend and *abide* (RSV

68

reads "remain"), this is he who baptizes with the Holy Spirit (1:33). The abiding of the Spirit is for John the sign that Jesus is the Son of God.

In the conversation that follows, Jesus sees two disciples of John "following," and he asks what they want. They reply, "Where are you *abiding*?" (1:38, "staying" in RSV). The RSV translation is unfortunate for two reasons. First, it does not make obvious the connection between this discussion and John's witness, and second, it implies that the disciples are only concerned about where Jesus is living, though the immediate conversation appears to justify such an interpretation. Jesus responds "Come and see." And, we are told, "They came and saw where he was *abiding*, and they *abode* with him that day, for it was about the tenth hour" (1:39). The surface reading, which the RSV encourages, is that because of the lateness of the hour, the two disciples of John spent the night with Jesus. But something much more is involved here. From this point on these two are no longer disciples of the Baptist, but are disciples of Jesus. With no further indication of making any decision, one of the two, Andrew, goes the next morning to his brother Peter, and makes the first confession of faith, "We have found the Messiah." Clearly, "abiding" here is much more than finding shelter for the night, it is a matter of relationship between these two and Jesus. It is their becoming disciples.

This same conversation has another word that carries much more than its surface meaning in this gospel. The paragraph opens with John the Baptist's witness to Jesus, and immediately it is said "The two disciples heard him say this, and they followed (*akolouthein*) Jesus" (1:37). On the surface it would only appear that they walked after him, but to follow Jesus in this gospel is to be a disciple, and to be a disciple is to abide in Jesus.

The next appearance of *menien*, at 3:36, helps us understand the deep significance of this term for the Fourth Evangelist. Here one reads ". . . he who does not obey the Son shall not see life, but the wrath of God *menien* (KJ, "abideth"; RSV, "rests") upon him." Brown comments that "the present tense indicates that the punishment has begun and will last."[5] *Menien* conveys the idea of a permanent relationship here.

The term next appears near the end of the story of the Samaritan woman. The Samaritans ask Jesus to stay (*menein*) with them, so he "stayed (*menein*) there two days. And many more believed because of his word" (4:40b-41). Almost all commentators regard this as having no more significance than its simple, surface meaning. Barrett is unusual when, in commenting on this verse, he reminds his readers that this term "in John often has a rich theological content and this may be not altogether out of mind here," but his qualifications seem to suggest otherwise.[6] Yet

> . . . the second clause can be read "and he fellowshipped with them two days and many believed because of his revelation." It seems entirely possible that the Evangelist is trying to say that just as a spiritual relationship developed between Jesus and the two disciples when they stayed with him for the remainder of the day, so a similar relationship developed when he spent two days with the Samaritans. The close relationship of *menō* and *logos* in this passage is, as Carpenter has shown, supporting evidence for such an interpretation.[7]

Menein and *logos* are again found together at 5:38, where Jesus charges the Jews saying "and you do not have his word abiding in you, for you do not believe him whom he has sent." This charge could be interpreted as meaning that the Jews are not familiar with the Torah, but "word" (logos) here is clearly not the Torah, but rather it is the revelation given in Christ. They do not have a spiritual relationship with God because of their lack of belief in Jesus.

"Abide" next appears at 6:27, where, in a dialogue about bread, Jesus urges the multitude: "Do not labor for the food that perishes, but for the food which endures (*menein*) to eternal life." The word "endures" is not an inappropriate translation for *menein* at this point, except it masks the fact that it represents a word that is so important to Johannine thought. "Food" (*brōsis*) is used ambiguously in this passage. In the first usage it means material food, but in the second it refers to spiritual food. In this passage the idea of the permanence of the relationship is stressed. An emphasis which, as noted earlier, is important to the meaning of "abiding" in John.

At 6:56 the Evangelist next speaks of "abiding" in words attributed to Jesus: "He who eats my flesh and drinks my blood abides (*menein*) in me, and I in him." The next verse grounds this in the relationship that exists between Jesus and God. A major emphasis of the Fourth Gospel is that because Christ is from the living Father, one who abides in Christ has eternal life. It is significant to trace the progression of this idea through the gospel to this point. The baptism by the Spirit, to which John the Baptist gave testimony, marked the beginning of a new relationship between Jesus and the Spirit.[8] When the disciples of John abide with the spirit-filled Jesus, they become disciples. Jesus abides with the Samaritans for two days and many believe. Because the Jews refuse an abiding relationship, they cannot find life, but here that relationship is opened to all. In the history of interpretation there has been a dispute as to whether "abiding" is a mystical union, an ethical one, or both[9]--with contemporary scholarship emphasizing that it is a union that does not compromise the separateness of God from the individual.[10]

> . . . it is important to note that this is a spiritual, and not a physical 'abiding.' Anything within the context that might suggest the physical is discounted by the statement 'It is the spirit that gives life, the flesh is of no avail.'[11]

At 7:9 "abide" seems to be used with no symbolic overtones, Jesus has told his brothers that, because his time has not yet come, he is not going to Jerusalem, "So saying, he remained in Galilee." This is one of several places in John where the word is used to indicate a continuing relationship with a place. The others are at 10:40; 11:16; 12:24, 34; 19:31.

"Abiding" is again used in a spiritual sense in the conversation between Jesus and some Jews in 8:31, 35. Jesus first tells them that if they "abide (RSV, "continue") in my word (*logos*), you are truly my disciples" (8:31). The RSV reading does not suggest any spiritual implications, but only a belief which is something more than of the moment. But as has already been noted, "word" means Jesus' total revelation, and discipleship is a spiritual relationship. The sentence could be paraphrased: "If you have an enduring relationship with my revelation, you are in relationship to me as I am to God." The sentence continues, in the next verse, to say that this relationship brings a knowledge of the truth and freedom. Clearly one is here in the realm of the spiritual.

The Jews, however, have trouble understanding Jesus and protest that they, as sons of Abraham, have never been in bondage to anyone. Jesus replies: "The slave does not abide (RSV, "continue") in the house for ever; the son abides (RSV, "continues") for ever. So if the Son makes you free, you will be free indeed" (8:35-36). Clearly the abiding here is a spiritual relationship, and the whole argument of the passage is to show the Jews that their dependence on a physical relationship is to no avail.

In another conversation with the Jews, following the healing of the man born blind, Jesus is represented as saying, "If you were blind, you would have no guilt; but now you that say, 'We see,' your guilt abides" (RSV, "remains"). Here again the verb represents a continuing relationship, but this time with a spiritual state, sin.

A continuing spiritual relationship, but this time in a positive sense, is found in the use of the verb at 12:46: "I have come as light into the world, that whoever believes in me may not abide (RSV, "remain") in darkness." The relationship with darkness--which in Johannine thought is evil, outside of relationship with God--is broken by relationship to Christ.

The high point for the idea of abiding comes in chapters 14 and 15. At 14:10 it expresses the union that exists between Jesus and the Father: ". . . the Father who abides (RSV, "dwells") in me does his works." The enduring spiritual relationship which, at 6:56, was said to exist between Jesus and the believer is here said to exist between Jesus and God.

The King James translation has "abide" at 14:16, ". . . he shall give you another Comforter, that he may abide with you for ever," but the best textual evidence shows that *menein* was not in the original Greek, and that the RSV translation, "to be with you for ever," is correct. The next verse, however, does have it, where the Spirit of truth "abides (RSV, "dwells") with you and will be in you." Many commentators see "dwells with you" as a promise of the Spirit's presence with the Johannine Church, and "will be in you" as a promise of its presence with individual believers.[12]

In the allegory of the vine and the branches, "abide" is used nine times in seven verses (15:4-10). The theme is that one who abides in Christ bears fruit, and one who does not abide in Christ must be cast out. Further:

> If the believer abides in Christ, and his words [hrēmata = teachings] abide in the believers, they can ask anything and it will be done. They are to abide in Jesus' love even as he abides in the Father's love, and this abiding is dependent upon the keeping of his commandments. Finally, they have, in verse 16, been chosen that their fruit should abide.[13]

In these same last discourses the idea of "abiding" appears in yet another place where it is usually overlooked because of the common English translations. In 14:2 Jesus promises "In my Father's house are many abiding places (RSV, "rooms")." The Greek word for "abiding place," *menē*, comes from the same root as *menein*. Barrett, who points out this relationship, goes on to suggest that it means "a permanent, not a temporary, abiding-place," and that "communion with God is a permanent and universal possibility."[14]

To abide in Jesus is to become his disciple. As Jesus abides in God, so his disciples abide in him. This abiding brings the abiding Spirit, who empowers the disciple and the church. The abiding is dependent on keeping Jesus' teachings and doing his commandments, and it results in having a permanent abiding place with God. How much the tremendous development of this idea is lost by variant translations given to the consistent Greek word!

Chapter VII Endnotes

1.   This section is heavily dependent on my *Ambiguous Words and Apparent Synonyms*, 372-383.

2.   Brown, *John I-XII*, 510.

3.   Minear, Paul S., *John: The Martyr's Gospel*. (N. Y.: Pilgrim Press, 1984), 93. Minear credits George B. Caird. *The Language and Imagery of the Bible* (Philadelphia: Westminster Press, 1980), 47.

4.   Brown, *John* I-XII,, *loc. cit.*

5.   *Ibid. Cf.* Barrett, *John*, *loc. cit.*

6.   Barrett, *loc. cit.*

7.   Maynard, *Ambiguous Words and Apparent Synonyms*, 374-375. Carpenter citation is to his *Johannine Writings, loc. cit.*

8.   Some have argued that this baptism was, for John, the time of the incarnation. This is not impossible, but is difficult of proof.

9.   This problem is well covered by Scott, *Fourth Gospel*, 293-294.

10.   Representative is Brown, *John I-XII*, 510-512. *Cf.* Hauck, "*menō*" in, Gerhard Kittel, ed., *Theological Dictionary of the New Testament* (Grand Rapids: Eerdmans, 1967), IV, 574-588.

11.   Maynard, *Ambiguous Words and Apparent Synonyms*, 377.

12.   Schnackenburg, *John*, III 76; and Lindars, *John*, *loc. cit.*, are representative. There is a textual problem about the future tense. It probably should be present--"is in you."

13.   Maynard, *Ambiguous Words and Apparent Synonyms*, 381.

14.   Barrett, *John*, *ad. loc.*

Chapter VIII

Jesus Has Returned!

The Synoptic Gospels look forward to the Second Advent of Jesus, an event which is usually associated with the resurrection of the dead and the Last Judgment. This eschatological hope is also prominent in the writings of Paul, but when one turns to the Fourth Gospel, these ideas are replaced by an emphasis on the mystical return of Jesus, the gift of the Paraclete (Comforter), eternal life, and the judgment as an event already accomplished.

The emphasis on the mystical return of Jesus and the gift of the Paraclete is found in the farewell discourse and prayer of chapters 14-17. The main emphasis of this passage is on the mystical return of Jesus. It is summed up in the words of 14:20, "In that day you will know that I am in my Father, and you in me, and I in you." True, there is in the opening part of the discourse a promise that Jesus will return to take his disciples to the place which he will prepare for them,[1] but the main emphasis is not on Jesus taking the disciples to heaven, but on Jesus joining the disciples here. In 14:18 one reads, "I will not leave you desolate: I will come to you"; in 14:21, "I will love him, and manifest myself to him"; in 15:4, "Abide in me, and I in you"; in 16:22, "I will see[2] you again and your hearts will rejoice"; in the priestly prayer, "that they may all be one; even as thou, Father, art in me, and I in thee, that they also may be in us" (17:21); "I in them, and thou in me (17:23a); "That the love with which thou hast loved me may be in them, and I in them (17:26b).

By the time the Evangelist wrote these passages, many within the church must have been weary of waiting for the return of Jesus. Paul, at least in his earlier epistles, was looking forward to the return within his life time, but Paul was now long since dead, and Jesus had not returned on any cloud let down from heaven. Was the hope for his return a false hope? No, says John, he has returned already, in mystical fellowship with his believers. John had experienced that sense of the indwelling presence of Jesus in his own life, and he makes what Jesus says about his return point to that mystical, spiritual relationship. The Greek of 16:16 subtly makes this emphasis by the choice of the words for "seeing." The old King James reads "A little while, and ye shall not see me: and again, a little while, and ye shall see me, because I go to the Father." In the Greek two different words are used for "seeing," the first, *theōreō* meant "to be a spectator of," the other, *horaō*, meant to see with spiritual comprehension. The passage might be paraphrased: "A little while, and you will no longer be spectators of my presence; but after that you shall spiritually discern my presence."

Closely interwoven with these passages dealing with the return of Jesus spiritually, is the promise of the Paraclete (Comforter).[3] This promise is made in four different passages, 14:15-17; 14:25-26; 15:26-27; and 16:5-15. Windisch, a German scholar, held that these passages form a unity, and that the farewell discourse is complete without them and interrupted by them.[4] Arguments regarding unity and interrupted thought are highly subjective. The present writer has carefully read the discourse without the Paraclete material and feels that the continuity is not too much broken by its omission. On the other hand, he has read the Paraclete material as a unit, and finds it impossible to get any sense of smooth continuity. If the Paraclete passages were written for later insertion into the discourse, they were not written as a unit, but were written to be inserted at the points where they are now found. It seems more probable that the passage was originally written about as it now stands.[5]

The Paraclete passages variously promise the Holy Spirit or the Spirit of truth, which will be with the disciples and aid them in much the same way as the returned Jesus will aid them. It seems highly probable that the Holy Spirit and the Spirit of truth are one and the same, and that John does not carefully distinguish between the Holy Spirit and the Spirit of Jesus, writing as he did before the development of a rigid doctrine of the trinity.[6] The Paraclete passages in any event do not stand in opposition to the main thought of the discourse, but supplement the promise of the Spirit of Jesus with that of the Spirit of God.

Since the hope for the resurrection from the dead was closely associated with the expected return of Jesus, John was confronted with the question: "If Christ has already returned, when will the dead rise?" His answer was in the expression, "eternal life," which begins not at some point in the future, but when one accepts Jesus. He made this point most forceably in the story of the resurrection of Lazarus. There Martha expresses not only the Jewish view but the dominate early Christian view, "I know that he shall rise again in the resurrection at the last day" (Jn. 11:24). To which Jesus replies: "I am the resurrection, and the life: he who believes in me, though he die, yet shall he live, and whoever lives and believes in me shall never die" (Jn. 11:25-26).

This emphasis on eternal life as beginning in this world, and not dependent upon a general resurrection at the last day, seems to be negated by the references to the resurrection "at the last day" found in 6:39, 40, 44, 54. The view expressed by this phrase is not only contradictory to the view of the Lazarus incident, but it is contradictory to the view expressed in 6:47-61. Many scholars have assigned it to a later editor because of this inconsistency. In addition to the doctrinal problem, it has been discovered that in these passages the words for "see" are used in a manner inconsistent with Johannine usage elsewhere,[7] suggesting that they have been subject to later editorial revision. It may well be that some later editor wanted to get support for the orthodox view of a resurrection at the last day before it was rejected in 6:47-51 and chapter 11, thereby trying to nullify the force of the rejection. This later editor could well have been the same person who wrote chapter 21, which had the same purpose of making the gospel more acceptable to non-Johannine churches.

Just as the Evangelist got away from the need for a second advent to provide a time for the resurrection by saying that eternal life had already begun, he makes it no longer necessary as a time for judgment, for that, too, has taken place. In 3:17-19 he says that God does not send his son into the world for judgment, but that judgment does take place. This is another passage where John's use of words is interesting. The word "to judge" meant also "to separate," and it is very probable that John has used the word with a double connotation. The passage might be paraphrased as follows:

> For God sent the Son into the world, not to judge the world, but that the world might be saved through him; but he who does not believe is already separated from him, . . . And this is the basis for the separation, that the light has come into the world, and men loved darkness rather than light.

In other words, the judgment, as John sees it, is not the arbitrary decision of Jesus, but it is the inevitable result of the choice of men. Practically the same idea is repeated at 12:44-50, where it is said that the word which Jesus speaks will judge a man, but the expression "at the last day" appears. The function of Jesus is not to judge, but to save, and men are judged by the revelation of God that he gives. The reference to "the last day" has been held to be a later insertion by such scholars as Bacon, Wendt, and Bultmann, while more recent scholars such as Barrett, Brown, Lindars, and Sanders and Mastin make no comment, and thus appear to accept it as from the Evangelist.[8] However, it is marked, like the other "last day" passages, by an un-Johannine use of the verbs "to see," and again the older commentators may be right. The passage may have undergone editorial revision to support the more orthodox view. But even if this passage is accepted, the Jesus of the Fourth Gospel is not a judge--persons judge themselves against the revelation of God which he gives.

The writer of the Fourth Gospel has dropped the apocalyptic eschatological hope of a return of Jesus on a cloud let down from heaven in favor of a return of Jesus which he has already experienced in his own life-- the mystical union of the Spirit with the believer. Paul could and did experience this mystical union and yet still look forward to an eschatological return, but the writer of the Fourth Gospel has experienced eternal life and has seen persons separating themselves from God by rejecting Jesus. Not only has Jesus returned already, but eternal life and judgment are present realities. There is no need to expect Jesus to come again. He has kept that promise already, and has performed the functions which usher in the new era. Undoubtedly the Evangelist, editor of the Good News which we have seen him to be, is here once more interpreting Jesus in terms of his own experience and the experience of his fellow Christians.

As to whether this interpretation was in line with what Jesus himself actually taught is a much more knotty problem. Certainly it is not in line with what Paul believed, and with what the Synoptics, at least in certain passages, believe Jesus to have taught. Yet the one point at which Jesus had the greatest difficulty in his ministry was to get people to understand the nature of his Kingdom. The conflicting views presented in the Synoptics leads one to wonder how accurately they represent the mind of the Master. The possibility remains that at this point John not only freed the Gospel for an essentially apocalyptic eschatology, but that he also more truly represented the great spiritual insights and emphases of Jesus.

Chapter VIII Endnotes

1.   Howard, in *Christianity according to St. John*, 74, considers this to be the main emphasis of the discourse, but it seems necessary to reject this, for the reasons indicated.

2.   *Horaö*, the word usually used in this gospel with the connotation of spiritual insight.

3.   "Comforter" is the most common translation of the Greek, but it does not do justice to the full meaning of the term, therefore I prefer to transliterate the Greek. A Paraclete was one who stood by another person in any situation. The terms had its origins in Greek legal practice, where it designated a person who acted much as a modern lawyer, but who had no particular legal training. It came to have the more general meaning indicated above.

4.   Windisch as summarized by Howard, *op. cit.*, 72ff.

5.   Major contemporary scholars regard these passages as from the Evangelist. Thus Schnackenburg (*op. cit.*, III, 74) writes "I shall therefore not follow any theory of interpolation." *Cf.* Lindars, *op. cit.*, 468.

6.   The use of the expression "another Comforter" in 14:16 has been held to militate against this suggestion, but the distinction there seems to be not between the Spirit of truth and the Holy Spirit, but between the physical Jesus who is now comforting his disciples, and the Spirit which shall take his place. This Spirit can be referred to either as a Paraclete or as the Spirit of truth.

7.   Maynard, *Apparent Synonyms and Ambiguous Words*, 247.

8.   Bultmann, *The Gospel of John: A Commentary*. trans. by Beassley-Murray, Hoare, and Riches (Philadelphia: Westminster Press, 1971), 345 n.6. For the more contemporary view, see Barrett, *op. cit.*, *loc. cit.*; Brown, *John*, *XIII-XXI*, loc. cit.; Lindars, *op. cit.*, loc. cit. and Sanders and Mastin, *The Gospel According to St. John*. Black's New Testament Commentaries (London: Adam & Charles Black, 1968), *loc. cit.*

Chapter IX

Summary and Concluding Thoughts

This study has presented the Gospel of John as the work of "the Evangelist" who was not John, son of Zebedee, one of the twelve disciples. His name is unknown. When, in this study he has been referred to as "John," that has simply been a matter of convenience. All one can say for sure about him is that he was a Jewish Christian leader of the church or small group of churches that were in conflict with the mainline churches of their day over issues of christology, authority in the church, the role of the Spirit and their understanding of the Second Coming. The Johannine churches were also in conflict with the Jewish synagogues of their communities. Apparently the members of these churches had once worshiped in the synagogue as well as in the church, but had found themselves expelled from the synagogue.

The location of this community is not clear. The only suggestion made in this study is that it may have been in Alexandria. The traditional location of Ephesus is not impossible, but due to the relation of that church to Paul, seems improbable. It seems clear that it was a church located outside of Palestine. The writer himself knows Greek very well and is conscious of the exact shade of meaning of various Greek words. He is also familiar with certain Greek concepts, of which the Logos (Word) may be the most important. On the other hand, he is also very familiar with the Old Testament, which he seems to use in Greek, and with Jewish methods of interpreting scripture and writing, including midrash, *inclusio* and chiastic

82

structure. It would seem possible that he was once trained as a Rabbi, but
that he had experienced a profound Christian conversion.

In his writing he was primarily concerned to interpret the Christian
tradition for the Church of his day. It is very possible that the material was
originally developed for use in preaching because the Old Testament
material seems to follow the Jewish lectionary, but if this is the case, the
book is much more than a collection of sermons; it is organized in a very
systematic fashion, introducing early ideas that will be developed later, and
the whole controlled by the concept of Jesus' hour. Therefore, while the
material may have been first developed for preaching, in its final form it
probably was intended to be read in the churches, along with the Jewish
lectionary readings.

The author had an exalted view of Christ as the pre-existent Logos
who had been with God from the beginning of creation, was the agent of
creation, and had become flesh as the child of Mary and Joseph. John must
have known the story of the virgin birth, if, as the present writer believes, he
knew and used the other gospels, but the manner of the birth of Jesus was
inconsequential to him; the important thing was that the word had become
flesh. This incarnate Christ had moved through his ministry as the divine
being, and had returned in glory, leaving behind his church, which he had put
under the control of a charismatic leadership, and to which he had entrusted
the whole revelation.[1]

This charismatic leadership, however, sometimes tended to put more
stress on the prophetic utterances of the present than on the teachings of
Jesus. This is always a problem for institutions that have charismatics in their
leadership. The Evangelist is not opposed to the gift of the Spirit, but it must
be controlled by the teachings of Jesus. That is the reason for the strong
emphasis on keeping Christ's commandments, words, and teaching found in
the gospel.[2]

The Johannine churches found their authority not in Peter nor James
the brother of Jesus (as in Acts), nor in any other of the twelve disciples, but
rather in the anonymous beloved disciple. The argument of this study has
been that this beloved disciple was probably *not* a historical figure. He was

rather any spirit-filled person who was in relationship to Christ as Christ is to God.

While this study has not examined them, the Johannine epistles, and especially III John, give additional insight into church organization in the Johannine community. These epistles do not, in the view of the present writer, come from the author of the Fourth Gospel. On the basis of word studies, I John may come from the Redactor who wrote chapter 21, and II and III John come from yet another author who calls himself "the Elder." The title is significant. In III John we find the Elder in conflict with one Diotrephes, who is exercising the authority of a bishop. It would appear that the Johannine community is controlled by elders, and that at least one of them is not only opposed to Petrine authority, but also to the move toward episcopal leadership in the church.

The Evangelist gives rather clear indication that he is opposed to any magical or "automatic" view of the sacraments. He deemphazies them by not telling of the baptism of Jesus nor of the institution of the Last Supper. Yet he has three, and possibly five passages which would suggest that the sacraments, spiritually understood, were important to him. The first is the first miracle where the new wine possibly represents the wine of the eucharist. If this symbolism is correct, then the eucharist replaces the Jewish water of purification as the mode of salvation.[3]

A much more important passage is the discourse that follows the feeding of the multitude. There, John has Jesus say, ". . .unless you eat the flesh of the Son of man and drink his blood, you have no life in you" (Jn. 6:53). This comment seems rather incongruous following a meal of bread and fish, but this may be a deliberate way of deemphasizing a materialistic view of the eucharist. Culpepper is undoubtedly correct when he says of this passage, "crass cannibalistic and magical interpretations of the Lord's supper are rejected."[4] John's understanding of the eucharist comes in the words "It is the spirit that gives life, the flesh is of no avail; the words that I have spoken unto you are spirit and life" (Jn. 6:63).

The third passage which reflects the Johannine understanding of the sacraments is 13:10, with its play on the words for "bathe" and "wash," which, as suggested above,[5] may indicate baptism and the eucharist. Found in the

setting where one would expect the institution of the eucharist, the stress is
on obedience and humble service. The thrust would seem to be that while
the mechanics of the sacraments are not to be ignored--Peter must be
washed following his having been bathed--it is obedient abiding in Christ that
is important.

The possible fourth sacramental reference is the scene at the cross,
where blood and water flow from the pierced side of Jesus (Jn. 19:34).
Bultmann suggests that the meaning here ".... can scarcely be other than that
in the death of Jesus on the cross the sacraments of baptism and the Lord's
Supper have their foundation."[6] Minear points out that this incident is the
fulfillment of the prophecy of Zechariah 12 and, more importantly, the
fulfillment of Jesus' own prophecies. The flow of water was predicted by the
promise of living water in 7:37-39, where there are interesting connections
with our present passage: Nicodemus is in both and both are on the great
day of a festival. The flow of blood was predicted by Jesus in the promise of
6:53-54, "whoever eats my flesh and drinks my blood has eternal life."
Minear, while not denying sacramental overtones, thinks the main thrust is
elsewhere:

> It would be in his dying that he would complete both his
> coming from the Father and his going to the Father. To drink
> his blood, therefore, is to receive life from him and to share in
> his vicarious dying. . . . Whoever drinks his blood becomes, like
> him, a seed falling into the ground. So interpreted, the two
> images are consistent: the drinking of water (chapter 7) and
> the drinking of blood (chapter 6). In both cases eternal life is
> made available through the continuing of Jesus' ministry after
> his death. Both predictions are fulfilled in the flow of blood
> and water from the side of the crucified, which the soldier had
> seen. . . . . For the narrator, the testimony of the soldier looked
> forward to similar miracles that would accompany later
> martyrdoms.[7]

The present writer believes that Minear has not made his case for the
emphasis on martyrdom in the gospel, and in any event, as Minear would
seem to agree, this verse can also have sacramental significance.

The final passage which seems to have sacramental overtones is 3:5:
". . . unless one is born of water and the Spirit, he cannot enter the kingdom
of God." Lindars has a very perceptive comment on this verse:

> It is not absolutely necessary to assume that John is referring to the Christian sacrament of baptism when he uses this phrase. The symbolism of water in connection with the Spirit is frequent in the OT (e.g. Ezek. 36.25f.) and in the Qumran texts (e.g. IQS iv.19-21) where the context requires spiritual cleansing and renewal, *cf.* also 7.37-39. But the impression that Christian baptism is meant is hard to resist. John is not concerned with the outward aspect of it, and so **water** plays no further part in the argument.[8]

Lindar's final sentence is an apt summary not only of the 3:5 passage, but of the Evangelist's total attitude toward the sacraments. The external observance of the sacraments has no significance unless they are accompanied by spiritual renewal. Perhaps we can say that John is a sacramentalist, but that he is anti-sacramentarian!

The aim of this study has been to face honestly and scientifically the Fourth Gospel, to discover with as much precision as possible the meaning which it had for its author, in order that we may better understand the message which he had for us. Most of the suggestions advanced have not been new. Indeed, some of them are passing out of current vogue, but the suggestions which have been advanced have in most instances been reenforced by new word studies, and taken in their entirety, they present a view of the gospel which is consistent. Because it has taken seriously the suggestion, which is at least as old as Origen, that this is a symbolical gospel which has sometimes used what Origen called "material falsehood" to preserve spiritual truths, there may be some who will feel robbed of cherished truth and left but with an empty husk. But others will find that they are freed from the problems of the obvious inconsistencies between this gospel and the Synoptics and left with a deeper appreciation not only of what Jesus meant to a great unknown Christian of the early second century, but of what he can mean to us.

Chapter IX Endnotes

1.   *Supra*, 15f., 60f.

2.   Minear, *op. cit.*, makes a strong case for the importance of this function for the gospel.

3.   *Supra*, 18.

4.   Culpepper, *op. cit.*, 197.

5.   *Supra*, 58.

6.   Bultmann, *op. cit.*. Bultmann holds that v. 34b comes from a redactor--a view not widely held today.

7.   Minear, *op. cit.*, 75-77. Quotation is from 77.

8.   Lindars, *op. cit.*, *loc. cit.*

INDEX OF BIBLICAL REFERENCES

Boldface type indicates the place a passage receives major treatment.

88

SUBJECT INDEX

Boldface type indicates the place a passage receives major treatment.

DATE DUE

NOV 2 8 1993		
DEC 2 6 1993		
DEC 1 9 1994		
MAY 1 1 1995		
AUG 2 9 2001		